Teaching Children to Write

Teaching Children to Write

CONSTRUCTING MEANING AND MASTERING MECHANICS

Daniel R. Meier

Teachers College, Columbia University
New York and London

National Writing Project
Berkeley, CA

Published simultaneously by Teachers College Press, 1234 Amsterdam Avenue, New York, NY 10027, and the National Writing Project, 2105 Bancroft Way, Berkeley, CA 94720-1042.

The National Writing Project (NWP) is a professional development network of more than 200 university-based sites, serving teachers across disciplines and at all levels, early childhood through university. The sites work in partnership with surrounding school districts across all 50 states, the District of Columbia, Puerto Rico, and the U.S. Virgin Islands. The NWP focuses the knowledge, expertise, and leadership of our nation's educators on sustained efforts to improve writing and learning for all learners.

The author would like to express gratitude for permission to use the following:

Rae Armantrout, "Reserved," excerpted from *Next Life* © 2007 by Rae Armantrout. Reprinted with permission of Wesleyan University Press.

Nate Koch, "Different Water," from *River of Words* © 2005 by River of Words. Reprinted with permission of River of Words.

Library of Congress Cataloging-in-Publication Data

Meier, Daniel R.
  Teaching children to write : constructing meaning and mastering mechanics / Daniel R. Meier.
     p. cm.
  Includes bibliographical references and index.
  ISBN 978-0-8077-5238-8 (pbk. : alk. paper)— ISBN 978-0-8077-5239-5 (hardcover : alk. paper) 1. Children—Writing. 2. Language arts (Elementary) I. Title.
  LB1139.W7M45 2011
  372.6'044—dc23

                                                                                    2011019095

ISBN 978-0-8077-5238-8 (paperback)
ISBN 978-0-8077-5239-5 (hardcover)

Printed on acid-free paper

Manufactured in the United States of America

18 17 16 15 14 13 12 11   8 7 6 5 4 3 2 1

for my father—

vivete fortes

CONTENTS

Acknowledgments   *ix*

Introduction   *1*

Integrating Meaning and
     Written Language Conventions   *2*
Toward a Writing Mind   *8*
Overview of the Book   *9*

1. Children's Early Writing Development   *13*

Thought and Language   *14*
Language and Writing Development   *16*
Writing Before Reading   *18*
Attention to Development   *21*
Writing as a Process   *24*
Sociocultural Perspectives   *26*
Literacy and New Language Learners   *28*

2. Content and Mechanics   *32*

What's Basic About Writing Well?   *33*
Constructing Knowledge   *36*

3. Planning   *52*

Theoretical Reminders   *53*
Potential Stumbling Blocks   *54*
Planning as Writing   *57*

Reading and Writing:
  Key Connections for Planning   73
Planning for Writing:
  It Can Start as a Speck   77

4. The Art of Composing   78
Composing and Authorship   79
Ideas and Strategies for Composing Well   81
Bringing Awareness to the Composing Process   85
Integrating Genres Across the
  Composing Curriculum   92

5. Editing and Revising   100
Challenges   100
Theoretical Foundations   102
Strategies for Editing and Revision   106

6. A Writing Mind   134
An Inventiveness With Mechanics   134
Originality and Creativity   136
The Evolving Teaching Mind   138

References   145

Index   149

About the Author   158

ACKNOWLEDGMENTS

I never remember how ideas come to me for writing a new book. I do know, though, that the drive to write and publish first started with Brian Ellerbeck from Teachers College Press. He was the only editor who picked up my first manuscript, and for that I will be forever grateful for his confidence in my writing. This is my 6th book with the Press, and I acknowledge and thank Brian for getting me started, which after all is key for finishing any kind of writing.

I also thank my editor Marie Ellen Larcada, who has patiently waited for this manuscript and encouraged me that it could get done. She also supported my goal of writing a book for K–4 educators and making a link across the lower and upper grades. Thanks, too, to the anonymous reviewers of my initial proposal as I reread their insightful comments as I wrote this book.

A huge thank you also to the child authors and their families who allowed me to use their comments and work in this book. Books on writing are always richer when we can hear children's voices and see their work, and I wish them the best in their writing careers. Thanks, also, to Louisa Michaels at River of Words for helping secure a permission to use a poem by Nate Koch, and also to Suzanna Tamminen at Wesleyan University Press for allowing me to reprint "Reserved" by Rae Armantrout.

I also thank Hazelle, Kaili, and Toby. Hazelle helped me find time to write and reminded me that I have something to say and that I can say it. Even after writing several books, it doesn't get any easier, and this book proved the hardest to write of all so far. Hazelle reminded me that I just need to keep doing what I have been doing when I write. Toby reminded me to keep it "simple" and Kaili allowed me to showcase some of her wonderful K–4 writing.

I also owe a profound thanks to the wonderful teachers featured in this book—Florence Tse, Sarah Carp, Joli Gordon, Amanda Abarbanel-Rice, Liz Goss, Ilsa Miller, and Madhuvanti Khare. They devoted time for an interview, edited what I wrote about them, helped me secure releases, and provided me with writing from their students and resources from their teaching. This is my first book that features such an extensive quoting of the views and experiences of teachers, and this is for sure one of the strengths of the book. Writing up their ideas and strategies gave me great joy and pride. I thank the teachers not only for their time and energy, but for their dedication to teaching writing and to the education of their children and their fellow educators.

I'd also like to acknowledge my own mentors in the field of writing and education. At Middlebury College's Bread Loaf School of English, I was fortunate to take classes with Dixie Goswami, John Elder, Shirley Brice Heath, Courtney Cazden, and John Dixon, and had the pleasure of hearing Jimmy Britton, Nancy Martin, Nancie Atwell, James Moffett, and Ken Macrorie talk about writing theory and practice. These are critical pioneers in writing research and teaching. I was also fortunate to spend a semester at Goldsmith's College in London, where I met Eve Gregory and Charmian Kenner. These two theorists provided me with an expanded international perspective on writing. I also acknowledge the work of Anne Haas Dyson, my doctoral advisor at the University of California at Berkeley, who showed me the power of linking theory and children's writing and looking broadly and deeply at what and how young children write.

I also thank Louise Rosenkrantz, Liz Goss, and Sarah Rosenthal for reading and commenting on emerging chapters from the book. It's always hard to find readers for 30-page chapters but these friends and colleagues did it with both good cheer and keen insight.

INTRODUCTION

Space Book

By Thyra (age 5, kindergarten)

(This book is dedicated to all the aliens in the world.)

The alien is in his space ship flying into earth.
The spaceship landed into my backyard.
I raced to my backyard to see what was going on.
I introduced him to the town.
We were friends.
All of my friends loved him.
I took him to school.
The alien's mom came to pick him up.
He was sad when he left.

How To Play Baseball

By Cristian (age 7, 2nd grade)

I'm going to teach you how to play baseball. The person behind home plate is called the catcher. If the catcher catches the ball 3 times, you're out. The umpire stands behind the catcher. There are 9 players on a team. When you're going to bat, a person throws a ball to you. You try to hit the ball. If you hit the ball, you run the bases. If you don't get a home run, wait until someone else hits the ball and try to get a home run. Now you know how to play baseball.

INTEGRATING MEANING AND WRITTEN LANGUAGE CONVENTIONS

Thyra and Cristian are two young writers who can help us see new ways to integrate content and mechanics in our teaching of writing. Their writing helps us look within and across grade levels at how we can re-examine and strengthen content and mechanics integration. Both young writers are working to increase the accuracy and creativity of their writing, and melding content and mechanics is a critical aspect of their goal of writing well.

Thyra, an experienced writer even in kindergarten, juggles a range of written language conventions and levels of meaning as she composes her book about aliens. An able speller for a kindergartner, Thyra's spelling is conventional enough for Thyra to read most of it back, and for her teacher to read it on her own. In terms of *mechanics*, Thyra's first draft showed a solid beginning control over the physical formation of letters, a range of sentence structures, varied verb tenses, mostly recognizable spelling and punctuation, the use of a dedication line, and repeated words and parallel phrases ("into the earth" and "into my backyard"). In terms of *content*, Thyra's story has an enticing story hook ("The alien is in his spaceship flying into earth"), sudden plot twists ("The spaceship landed into my backyard"), inventive language and action ("I introduced him to the town"), and a story arc of action and resolution (alien comes to earth, has a set of adventures with an earthling, and returns home with his mom). In Thyra's story, these elements of mechanics and content work together in an integrated way as she creates an inventive, flowing, and lively little story. Thyra could write at this level because of her talents as a language and literacy learner, and also because of her kindergarten teacher, who provided both open-ended and focused opportunities to integrate written language content and mechanics.

Cristian, a 2nd-grader whose first language is Spanish, also undergoes a similar juggling act as he composes his "how to" book on playing baseball. As I worked with him (as a classroom volunteer), I helped scaffold and support both the content and mechanics of his piece. I provided help with some spelling, and wrote some sentences as he dictated to me, and I nudged him along with content questions and prompts. In terms of *mechanics*, Cristian carefully sounded out the words as he tried to spell as many words as he could, varied his sentences as he wrote and dictated to me, worked hard to make his writing legible, added varied verb tenses, used contractions ("I'm" and "you're"), and repeated certain words ("If you hit the ball . . . ," "If you don't get a home run . . .") for alliterative effect.

For *content*, Cristian has a wonderful opening line to hook the reader in ("I'm going to teach you how to play baseball"), excellent information about baseball as he explains key positions ("The person behind the plate is called the catcher") and logistics ("If you hit the ball, you run the bases"), makes up his own rules ("If the catcher catches the ball 3 times, you're out"), includes the reader/audience and anticipates possible scenarios ("If you don't get a home run, wait until someone else hits the ball and try to get a home run"), and in an overall way shows a masterful understanding of the format or genre of a "how to" piece of informational writing.

Thyra and Cristian both had the same teacher since she changed grade levels from kindergarten to grade 2. The teacher, Amanda Abarbanel-Rice, is one of the wonderful teachers of writing and literacy featured in this book. Thyra thrived in Amanda's classroom because she was provided with freedom and independence to write as she saw fit—to meld her knowledge of content and mechanics around both open-ended and semi-structured writing routines and activities. As a highly capable writer in kindergarten, Thyra was afforded the writing and creative space to extend and nudge herself along in terms of linking content and conventions in new and inventive ways. Amanda acted as guide and facilitator, keenly aware of Thyra's talents and nurturing her in baby steps along the way to extend and grow her writing. Cristian, as a new language learner (Gregory, 2008) acquiring a second language, also benefited from Amanda's talent for blending open-ended and semi-structured writing actities and projects within predictable and stimulating daily routines for writing. As seen in the example above, Cristian, like other new language learners, benefits from close and sustained adult support with mechanics and content, and in linking and integrating these two areas. He also benefited from the format or structure of the writing activity, composing a "how to" piece, because it gave him an overall frame for writing an informational picture of how to play baseball. Cristian also benefited from his background knowledge of baseball, and from his own literary talent for addressing the reader in a conversational way and for creatively inventing new information about baseball.

What's the value of integrating content and mechanics in writing? The elementary school years are a crucial period for inculcating lifelong habits and dispositions toward writing, and for children to learn sophisticated ways to create powerful, engaging, and masterful writing. It's a pivotal period in their writing lives to learn how to write with skill, accuracy, style, and originality. It is also a time when some students are already hesistant or reluctant writers—they don't think they have anything to say and write and/or they don't feel they know how to write well enough. When children are provided with inspired and enriching writing instruction that integrates content and mechanics through thoughtful, well-planned, and reflective teaching, students become competent and powerful writers in terms of what they write, how well they say it, and how they view themselves as writers.

In much of the current literacy policy and curriculum nationwide, mastery of written language conventions is emphasized through whole-group direct instruction, scripted curriculum, and testing and assessment. There are certain important benefits to this emphasis, as the use of whole-class instruction can create a community of writers and thinkers, direct instruction can reach and support certain kinds of learners, scripted curriculum can provide a foundational framework, and assessment can provide useful data to inform writing instruction. But the wholesale application of these elements is detrimental to the short- and long-term goals of children writing well and the goal of teachers teaching writing well. Why? It oversimplifies conceptually what it takes for children to write well and waters down in a practical way what it takes for us to teach writing with effectiveness and power. It also cuts into the amount of time devoted to sustained, enriching writing instruction and actual writing in classrooms, and puts too high a premium on rote, low-level written language mechanics. As one of the anonymous reviewers of the proposal for this book so aptly noted, "Writing instruction that focuses purely on mechanics and skills has turned so much of the population off to writing, however an approach that ignores the need to teach conventions can privilege certain children over others. We need to find a way out of the false dichotomy." By rethinking and revising how we envision content and mechanics, and how we integrate the two in structured and creative ways in our teaching, we take our teaching to a higher level and also raise the accuracy, fluency, and power of children's writing.

Mastery of written language conventions is essential for writing well. It's part of the accuracy and inventiveness in writing well. There is no long-lasting sense of achievement and personal triumph if children do not gain control over a range of written language conventions across varied writing tasks. Most children in the early grades only gather enough momentum and motivation to write something of interest to themselves and to others when they feel they have a certain level of knowledge of and control over selected written language conventions. Effective writing instruction, then, emphasizes both a solid foundation in written language mechanics and interesting content with room for individual flair, voice, and passion.

It also fosters a sense of control and writing power for young writers, equipping them with the talents to both recognize and invent new content and mechanics since both are malleable elements. Our greatest writers are those who can control and internalize content and mechanics integration, and at the same time invent and create a never-before-seen integration that puts a new stamp, a new mark, on our body of writing and our conception of what it means to write well.

What are the key elements in written language *mechanics* that young writers need to experience, grapple with, control, incorporate, and learn?

Based on my work with children, my conversations with the talented teachers featured in this book, and influential research and theory, the following are essential written language elements to be learned over varied periods of development:

- the physical formation of alphabetic letters or other written symbols and characters
- transfering between the syntax of oral language and the syntax of written academic and literary language
- control over pauses and stops in daily speech and pauses and stops in written language
- recognizing and internalizing sound-symbol correspondence
- generating both spelling approximations and accurate word spellings both in isolation and within writing tasks
- transfering knowledge back and forth between writing in a first language and writing in a second language
- increasing knowledge of word meanings and incorporating that knowledge into written texts
- recognizing and distinguishing varied written language formats and genres
- flexibility in mixing and matching varied written language formats and genres
- recognizing and distinguishing elements of an author's style
- imitating and incorporating elements of an author's style into one's own writing

Each one of us can compose our own list or group of "essential" written language conventions, and rather than seeing this as a weakness in our writing instruction, it should be viewed as a potential source of strength and power in how and why we teach writing. I offer the above grouping as a springboard for us to mix and match our own most prized written language conventions, and for each of us to hone the list to support our particular students and our particular teaching situations. Regardless of the literacy or writing program or curriculum adopted by our school or district, we must *know and articulate* what it means to write well and deepen our understanding of powerful and transformative writing instruction. These two touchstones—knowledge of powerful writing and knowledge of powerful teaching—must always remain constant. The playwright Neil Simon has said, "The good mechanic knows how to take a car apart. I love to take the human mind apart and see how it works" (Lahr, 2010, p. 71). For us, as teachers of writing, identifying language conventions is a process of taking language apart and breaking it down for ourselves and for our students.

Written language conventions are the "tangibles" of learning to write well—they are the elements most easily visible and recognized by the human eye and ear for both children and adults. As Madhuvanti Khare, one of the teachers featured in this book observes, written language mechanics are also more "quantifiable" and easily counted for children.

Written language content and meaning are the "intangibles" of learning to write well—they are more slippery, harder to catch, and hold both for students and teachers. And yet it is valuable also to delineate a group of these intangibles as key elements for writing well for young writers:

- to gain the requisite motivation to write something of value and import
- to gain the confidence to take risks and try learning new written language forms
- to feel confident enough to make mistakes
- to have pride and excitement about one's writing
- to feel free enough not to get stuck doing only certain kinds of writing
- to feel and believe that one has something important to say both for oneself and others, and for audiences both real and imagined
- to be open to new forms of inspiration for improving one's writing
- to acquire and develop a personal signature style
- to know and reflect upon one's strengths and areas to modify
- to gain a sense of ownership
- to have a sense of voice as a writer and as an individual
- to be open to indirect and direct guidance and support from peers and adults
- to gain resiliency when encountering a writing setback
- to gain persistence with one piece of writing and the patience to let the right ideas and words develop

As Anne Frank wrote in her diary on April 5, 1944, 2 months before she and her family were arrested (Metselaar & van der Rol, 2004):

When I write I can shake off all my cares. My sorrow disappears, my spirits are revived! But, and that's a big question, will I ever be able to write something great, will I ever become a journalist or writer? I hope so, oh, I hope so very much, because writing allows me to record everything, all my thoughts, ideals, and fantasies. (p. 151).

When children write well, the two groups of elements are not in isolation, but exist in a dynamic and interwoven relationship with each other.

Over time, with our direct and indirect guidance, young writers learn to orchestrate an expanding repertoire of ways to dip into their two sets of elements in an integrated and connected way. This essentially developmental process occurs over a long period of children's linguistic, cognitive, cultural, and social growth. It does not always know or follow the artificial boundaries of a school year or a scope and sequence for mastery according to a certain timetable. And yet this is what we are asked to do in current writing instruction, and so we need to interweave the two sets of elements across the length of our writing time with a particular group of children.

Although I have separated out mechanics and content so we can break down their key elements for instructional purposes, there are critical ways that content and mechanics are inseparable and closely aligned. For example, haiku (three lines of 5 syllables, 7 syllables, and 5 syllables) and tanka (5 lines and a total of 31 syllables) are ancient forms of traditional Japanese poetry. The conventions and content of this poetry are intimately connected with their content, often nature and small moments of human life and experience.

Now that we've broken down key elements of written language mechanics and content, what are powerful ways that we can integrate the two for young writers? We first need a foundation that promotes effective and long-lasting literacy learning by providing direct and indirect opportunities for young writers to:

- write on a daily basis from the beginning to the end of the school year, and over the summer
- have ample time to plan, write, and revise
- revisit and reread their writing
- listen to the ideas, thoughts, and texts of other young writers
- link reading and writing experiences
- learn the styles and imprint of individual authors
- learn a range of written language genres and forms
- have access to oral language and social interaction as a permanent foundation rather than just an initial scaffold for writing
- have access to drawing and art as an additional foundation for writing
- receive developmentally appropriate support and guidance at a particular moment of writing
- develop a love of words and a love of language
- have access to their home and community traditions for using language and literacy

When we have these elements in place, we can then mix and match strategies for promoting an integration of content and mechanics for young writers.

The power in children's writing comes, bit by bit over time, when elements of mechanics are integrated with elements of meaning. I recently heard the composer Stephen Sondheim, at age 80, reflect on his long career writing musicals. When asked about his process for writing his lyrics and his music, Sondheim explained that he does not compose his musicals by first writing the music and then the lyrics, or vice versa. Rather, he writes a little music, and then adds in lyrics, then a little more music and then a little more lyrics, and so on until he creates an entire musical.

This is a helpful process for us to remember—that writing is essentially an artful dance that always seeks an integration and fusion of content and mechanics. We ask children to write in schools because it is an essential part of a good education. Writing empowers the soul, informs the mind, changes society and human action, and creates memories and ideas and images of great internal and external beauty and perfection. Well-told stories, provocative essays, poignant letters, informative reports, and passionate poetry—all hold some well-balanced mix of content and mechanics that give shape and substance and power to the written word.

TOWARD A WRITING MIND

A focus on content and mechanics integration puts us on the path of developing "a writing mind"—a habit of looking for and reflecting on ways to orchestrate children's writing talents and needs. It also involves seeing ways to break language down for children and also to put it back together again. Like the natural processes of composition and decomposition, it provides a framework for continually creating and taking apart words, sounds, ideas, feelings, and information in a myriad of different configurations and shapes. A key element in this kind of growth for us is a deeper understanding of the child mind in this process.

> Child mind is human mind. Its contents are different from adult mind because it has had less time to gather information, to gain knowledge from experience, to develop certain kinds of thinking and means of expression. And, probably because it is not yet completely acculturated, it is more of a world mind in the sense that it is open to trying options that other cultures have developed. . . . (Bissex, 1996, p. 126)

As part of a "world mind," young writers are learning the culture of writing and of learning to write in a school-based setting. We need, then, to understand the writing mind of young writers, and to carve out for ourselves a larger place in our educational philosophy and instruction for helping children integrate written language conventions and meaning.

The movement toward an ever more sophisticated writing mind for children begins with our understanding and support for almost untold complexities of learning to meld content and mechanics. For example, when kindergartners learn to write their names, they must orchestrate almost a dozen different elements of mechanics: adjust and hold onto the paper so it won't slide or move, hold the pencil or pen with a reasonably successful grip, find a good place to start on the page and decide on a direction in which to write, remember that in English writing goes from left to right and has a return sweep, remember or just choose a letter to start with, form that letter (upper- and/or lowercase) as a fine-motor activity, remember or randomly choose a next letter, and then repeat this whole sound-symbol/small-motor/cognitive/linguistic process until their name is written accurately or to the best of their developmental capabilities.

In this small example, children must account for almost a dozen written language elements *as if* these elements were a continuous developmental string. But they are not. So we must break down these elements for children, lay them out on the table as a feast for the writing senses, while at the same time engaging and leading children *as* they write and draw and talk and look at books. We then help children go back and forth between the *experience* of writing and where our experience is taking us at the moment and will just about take us (the message, meaning, understanding). This often less-than-graceful dance can make for a difficult teaching process (for us) and a difficult learning process (for children). We need, then, a sharply informed "writing mind" for planning and directing rich and masterful writing experiences, while also paying attention to showing children how to break down critical elements of content and mechanics.

Writing conventions and mechanics are often more highly prized in the mechanics/content ratio; they are simply easier to see and easier to assess and easier therefore to "teach." Yet, they are ultimately not easier to teach because the mechanics in question are only as good as the content and the meaning of a particular piece of writing. The mechanics only work as they are linked with creative content, a lively voice, a sense of audience and purpose—in short, writing that matters to self and audience. So our central pedagogical challenge, as well as our teaching joy, is to snap together mechanics and content whenever we can. It's like reaching into a bin of loose LEGOs and finding just the right piece to add to 25 different LEGO creations. We work toward placing relevant written language elements along developmental paths that create fluency and authenticity in writing.

OVERVIEW OF THE BOOK

In this book, I present ideas and strategies that help us conceptualize and promote an integration of written language content and mechanics in the primary grades. I explain key theory on early literacy research, the integration of content and mechanics, and effective teaching strategies. The book will appeal to new teachers who want to formulate their writing philosophy and curriculum in terms of content and mechanics. It will also appeal to experienced teachers, who want to refine and deepen their understanding and knowledge of how and why to integrate written language content and mechanics. The book will also interest teachers, literacy coaches, early literacy researchers, teacher educators, and parents.

Chapter 1 provides an overview of central research and ideas on children's early writing development over the last 40 years. I highlight key pioneers in writing research and pedagogy, and take a chronological approach to show how certain ideas and practices have taken shape over the last 4 decades. Chapter 2 looks at how we can define written language mechanics and content. Chapter 3 examines planning for writing, and relevant ideas and strategies for thinking about and preparing for writing. Chapter 4 looks at the composing process, the power of the first draft in writing, and effective support during writing for integrating content and mechanics. Chapter 5 examines revision and editing, and particular ways to use this process for paying more attention to melding content and mechanics. Chapter 6 closes the book and offers concluding ideas for sharpening and deepening our writing mind for understanding and teaching written language content and mechanics.

Chapters 2 through 6 feature ideas and strategies from several practicing teachers who are exemplary teachers of writing. I also add my own work with kindergarten-age children. The seven featured teachers have all taught more than one grade level in the K–4 range; teach children from varied cultural, linguistic, and economic backgrounds; and represent a range of writing philosophies and techniques regarding the integration of content and mechanics. These chapters refer back to key theory from Chapter 1 and also provide additional theory and ideas for each chapter's focus.

I feature the teachers in this book so that we can begin the conversation about content and mechanics integration, and begin picking and choosing those ideas and strategies to add to our particular writing philosophies and teaching contexts. Florence Tse has taught for 10 years and recently taught at Sherman Elementary School in the San Francisco Unified School District, where she taught mostly first-generation Chinese-American kindergartners in an ELD (English Language Development) classroom. Liz Goss has taught kindergarten, 1st, and 2nd grades for 9 years on Chicago's West Side, teaching 4 years at a Chicago public school and 5 years at Legacy Charter School in Chicago. Ilsa Miller has taught kindergarten and 1st grade for 9 years, and currently teaches 1st grade at the San Francisco Friends School in San Francisco. Amanda Abarbanel-Rice has taught kindergarten for 10 years and 2nd grade for 4 years, and currently teaches 2nd grade at Thousand Oaks Elementary School in Berkeley, California. Joli Gordon, an 11-year veteran, teaches 3rd grade at Clarendon Elementary School in the San Francisco Unified School District. Madhuvanti Khare has taught for 13 years and currently teaches 3rd grade at Berkeley Arts Magnet Elementary school in the Berkeley Unified School District. Sarah Carp is a Spanish/English bilingual educator who has taught for 8 years, and currently teaches the English half of a 4th-grade dual-immersion (English/Spanish) class at Buena Vista Elementary School in the San Francisco Unified School District.

I spoke informally with these seven teachers, and used a collection of questions as the basis for our discussions.

1. How would you define *mechanics* in teaching writing to students at your grade level?
2. How would you define *content* in teaching writing to students at your grade level?
3. What does it mean to you to "integrate" or find a "balance" between mechanics and content in teaching writing at the primary grade level?
4. What are the greatest challenges and joys in integrating mechanics and content?
5. In general, where do you get your best ideas for teaching writing?
6. In general, where do you get your best strategies for teaching writing?
7. How do you stay passionate and engaged in improving how and why you teach writing?

I sent the list of questions to the teachers ahead of our conversation, and some teachers either emailed me some responses before we spoke, or wrote down some notes on their own and referred to the notes as we spoke. I spoke with a few teachers in their classrooms, and several teachers referred to samples of children's writing and their teaching materials as examples as we spoke. I audiotaped almost all of the interviews and also took written notes. Molly Van Houten, a graduate student at San Francisco State University, expertly transcribed most of the interviews. I then reviewed the transcripts and looked at how the teachers define and envision content and mechanics, and their ideas and strategies for integrating content and mechanics for children at different age levels and with different backgrounds. When I finally wrote up their interview material in the chapters in this book, I sent the material to the teachers to review and comment on.

I extensively quote the teachers in this book because I want to give voice to their inner teaching minds and to their outer teaching strategies. In writing research and practice, and in education reform in general, we need to hear the voices of teachers—their ideas, discoveries, strategies, paths of learning, future hopes. Their voices provide new models of teachers thinking and reflecting and working toward deepening instructional knowledge and improving teaching practices. We can use their words as mirrors for reflecting upon our own philosophies and teaching.

Chapter 1

CHILDREN'S EARLY WRITING DEVELOPMENT

My First House

(This book is dedicated to my dad.)

This is my first house. There were the burglar's footprints there. He stepped in paint. Then the burglar stepped into my house. He got paint all over the furniture. My dad and me went home. We saw the footprints and the burglar. My dad picked up the burglar and threw him out. The burglar never came back.

—Fabian, Grade 1

As I helped Fabian write "My First House," he and I did a dance of deciphering where he wanted the story to go and getting "just enough" mechanics in place so we could both follow the unfolding story. In thinking about the significance of this developmental moment in Fabian's writing, it's helpful to know about key ideas in early writing research and theory. In this chapter, then, I present central ideas in children's early literacy learning and especially emphasize children's writing development.

Writing research and curriculum has blossomed over the last 40 years. It is no longer a new field, but it is still relatively young. We now know quite a bit about how and why children between the ages of 5 and 10 learn to write, and we know more about how and why we can effectively teach writing. We now know the value of paying more attention to both the process and product of writing, devoting more time to teaching writing, and we see children as more competent and creative writers capable of making informed choices in terms of content and mechanics.

In this chapter, I take a chronological and historical approach to tell the story of critical early literacy research and practice. In doing so, I highlight the ideas and work of a number of important theorists and practitioners. Most of the material that I cover is from the United States, although I include some from Russia, Mexico, Spain, the United Kingdom, and New Zealand.

THOUGHT AND LANGUAGE

In this section, I present ideas from the great Russian theorist Lev Vygotsky, whose translated works (1978, 1986) help us see the power of linking talk and interaction with internal mental operations and children's capabilities for writing.

Lev Semyonovich Vygotsky

Vygotsky (1978, 1986) helps us understand the developmental underpinnings of knowledgeable and sophisticated writing instruction. He helps us see the value of linking thought, writing, language, and social interaction. His ideas also help us see how learning to write, and to write well, is essentially a lifelong process of learning to control and manipulate writing as a symbol system. For Vygotsky, young children grow and develop along a continuum of using gestures, signs, oral language, and written language in ever more complicated ways. Along the way, play and interaction with peers, older children, teachers, and family members stimulate and enrich children's learning and development.

What's wonderful to remember about Vygotsky's ideas on language and thought is his emphasis on the dynamic nature between what children learn and do outside of their minds and bodies with others, and what happens internally in their minds. For Vygotsky, children's use of signs (an object representing or standing for another object) and tools (an object used to change reality) perform mediating (the active changing of reality through human behavior) functions in the development of children's thinking and understanding. We use tools, such as our own hands, as a way to focus and change the object or goal of a particular activity. Using Vygotsky's language, tools are thus "externally" oriented (1978, p. 55). Signs, such as human speech, do not change or alter external realities like tools do; rather, sign use is a "means of internal activity aimed at mastering oneself" (1978, p. 55). Signs are thus "internally" oriented.

According to Vygotsky, the prehistory of written language follows this course: Undifferentiated marks grow into scribbles and other symbolizing marks, then into figures and pictures, and finally into signs. Children move from first- to second-order symbolism when "they discover that they can draw not only things but speech" (1978, p. 115). The relationship between thought and speech is complex and intricate, and both are involved in a dynamic, ever-changing relationship evolving over time. As "thought changes into speech" it undergoes a number of transformations, for it "does not merely find expression in speech—it finds its reality and form" (1986, p. 219). As for language in action, or speech in social situations, "it is not sufficient to understand" someone else's words; we "have to understand his thought" (1986, p. 253). It is children's "inner speech" that is the fertile ground for so much internal thinking, guessing, hypothesizing, and planning. And when children's inner speech becomes linked with their external social speech, their linguistic and cognitive development begins to grow and soar.

Also central to Vygotsky's (1978) work is his notion of a zone of proximal development (ZPD), which is an "area" between what children can do independently and what they can accomplish with the aid of an adult or more capable peer. The first level is the "actual developmental level" as shown by children's performance in "already completed developmental cycles" (1978, p. 85). Social interaction, primarily in the form of problem-solving, is the main "vehicle" for "awakening a variety of internal developmental processes" (p. 90). Teaching and guided social interaction encourage children's developmental processes, which result in zones of proximal development.

So, for writing instruction, children experience a series of ZPDs, some trailing behind and some ahead in their realm of developmental capabilities. For example, children's understanding and control over voice in their writing may well have a long ZPD trail, as children need years to increase their understanding and use of ever more sophisticated strategies for writing with a strong and creative sense of voice. Other writing elements, such as punctuation, may have ZPDs with a shorter life span—as we ask children to pay particular attention to one kind of punctuation for a short period of time.

Vygotsky's ZPD notion has been adopted by others and popularized in the notion of "scaffolding," a dialogic process in which an adult or more capable peer assists with problem-solving tasks and activities (Cazden, 1988). We can think of the ZPD as

> . . . an area of ability for which one's previous achievements have prepared one, but which awaits assisted performance for its realization. That assistance may take the form of teacher/student interaction, or peer tutoring, or group activity—as well as the give and take of social cooperation in and out of school. (Britton, 1987, p. 25)

For writing instruction, then, the ZPD helps us think about teaching along a continuum of thinking, planning, writing, rewriting, rethinking, sharing—providing us with an underlying developmental process to consider what, when, and how to pinpoint and teach elements of content and mechanics.

In the rich tableau of our contemporary K–4 classrooms—varied in social and cultural traditions toward language and literacy, and children's experiences with literacy in and out of school—it's helpful to see a variety of zones of proximal development. So rather than applying one zone to a group of 20 1st-grade children's integration of content and mechanics, we need to conceptualize a range of zones befitting individuals and groups of children. For ourselves as educators, we too have our own internal zones for teaching writing—we teach best when we constantly adjust our views and strategies for content and mechanics integration based on the children's writing and our professional development.

LANGUAGE AND WRITING DEVELOPMENT

In the 1970s and 1980s prominent theorists from the United Kingdom (James Britton, Nancy Martin, John Dixon, Leslie Stratta, and others) put forth important ideas on linking language and writing development. In this section, I highlight the work of James Britton.

James Britton

James Britton's (1970, 1982) ideas on writing were inspired in part by the work of Lev Vygotsky, as Britton emphasized the power of language and interaction for supporting and guiding children toward internalizing critical elements of learning to write.

> . . . even as mature users of language we go to talk as a first stage when a task achieves more than a certain degree of difficulty. In practical terms, then, all that the children write, your response to what they write, their response to each other, all this takes place afloat a sea of talk. Talk is what provides the links between you and them and what they have written, between what they have written and each other. (Britton, 1970, p. 29)

This "sea of talk" provides a nurturing and sustaining home for children's rich and lively discussion about written texts, about the composing process, about revision, and about their lives as writers within a community of writers, talkers, and thinkers.

For Britton (1982), learning to write well involves much more than simple, direct instruction in written language forms and genres. It involves a deep level of internalization of written language forms that children come to know through rich language and reading experiences both in and out of school. For Britton, children internalize language forms from the world outside of themselves "[L]anguage is . . . outside in the world, not in the child. He has to internalize it in order to speak" (1982, p. 99). Britton saw a parallel process for learning to write. "There is another internalizing job when it comes to the written form . . . it [the internalization process] is highly selective and it depends upon internal structures already in existence" (1982, p. 99). This is why skilled and powerful writing comes from skilled and powerful reading and conversation—the act of writing activates already internalized "patterns of the written language" (1982, p. 98) that children call upon with spontaneity, accuracy, and fluency.

Britton (1970, 1982) also placed special emphasis on how children spontaneously shape their words, thoughts, and syntactical structures both in oral and written language.

> [W]riting allows time for premeditation; there is a gap between the forging of the utterance and its reception. Because of this premeditation, because we can work on the writing until we are satisfied with it, I think that the shaping process in writing is a sharper one that it is in talking. (1970, p. 30)

Learning to write, then, involves the challenge (and the joy) for children of integrating and coordinating their internal powers of thought with the experiential process of writing, and this integration is helped along by talk and social interaction.

"Shaping at the point of utterance"(Britton, 1982, p. 139), another key Brittonian idea, refers to composing and creating both word meanings and syntactical structures in talking and writing. When we provide children with opportunities for shaping varied ideas (content) in varied ways (mechanics) through *both* talking and writing, then we promote a rich transfer between oral and written language. For Britton (1982), this shaping has a cognitive dimension.

> I want to associate spontaneous shaping, whether in speech or writing, with the moment by moment interpretative process by which we make sense of what is happening around us; to see each as an instance of the pattern-forming propensity of man's mental processes. Thus, when we come to write, what is delivered to the pen is in part already shaped, stamped with the image of our own ways of perceiving. But the intention to share, inherent in spontaneous utterance, sets up a demand for further shaping. (p. 141)

Powerful writing instruction allows for "shaping at the point of utterance" in both speech and writing, and also the additional cycle of "sharing" that leads to deeper levels of "shaping." Britton reminds us that when children share their writing in a deep way, they engage in a continued process of shaping internally (in the writing mind) and externally on paper (in the experience of writing). This is a deep way of embedding children's writing in the social and intellectual life of a classroom, and places a powerful emphasis on the process of writing and thinking.

WRITING BEFORE READING

In the 1970s, an area of U.S. research looked at the benefits of young children learning to write before learning to read. The primary pioneers were Charles Read (1971, 1981), Carol Chomsky (1971), and Glenda Bissex (1980). Their approaches built on earlier and the then current thinking about children as active discoverers of patterns in their thinking and language. Their work contributed to early and influential ideas on "invented" and "temporary" spelling (Cambourne & Turbill, 1987), which were later called "transitional" and "developmental" spelling.

Charles Read

Read (1971, 1981) called the early spelling efforts of young writers "invented spelling," and argued that although children do not have a deep awareness of standardized spelling or "correct" language forms, they do have their own logical ways of matching sounds to alphabetic symbols. For Read (1981), when children are allowed and encouraged to take active stances in their literacy learning, their actual writing more closely approximates their writing development.

> . . . we need to define more precisely *where children are* [original emphasis] as they embark on reading and writing, that is, what expectations and assumptions they hold, what levels of representation they find natural, and how these starting points may differ from their ultimate destinations. (p. 106)

Read's work on children's approximations of correct spelling show that children have unconscious knowledge of certain sound-symbol patterns and links from their biological knowledge of language (Richgels, 2001). Read (1971) also revealed how children's invented spelling can be systematic, although these rules and patterns are not necessarily the same as the rules of standard or conventional spelling.

> What the children do not know is the set of lexical representations and the system of phonological rules that account for much of standard spelling; what

they do know is a system of phonetic relationships that they have not been taught by their parents and teachers. (p. 30)

Forty years later, Read's work on children's approximate spellings reminds us of the value of rich language talk as a foundation for children's spelling development.

Carol Chomsky

Carol Chomsky (1970) also looked at children's early spelling and language knowledge.

> Children have enormous phonetic acuity and ability to analyze words into their component sounds. Their analyses reflect their own linguistic organization of the phonetic material and do not always coincide with the way adults hear. (p. 296)

For Chomsky, children aged 5–8 use their growing knowledge of word sounds and patterns to spell, and this word bank helps children learn to write before they learn to read conventionally. Chomsky advocated "using letter sets or writing by hand (if the child can form letters)" (p. 296) as an important early process for mastering correct spelling and learning to read. The next step is for children to "look" at the words and try to "recognize" them, and often children try to "work it out sound by sound, the reverse of the process by which they wrote it" (p. 296). She argued that teachers can work closely with children and "expect their spellings to reflect" children's "own pronunciation and linguistic judgments" (p. 296) rather than teachers'. If children's spellings "bear little resemblance to conventional spelling," there is time later for correction—at this early stage, children are "busy using information from their own consciousness as to how words sound" (p. 296).

Forty years later, it is helpful to look again at Chomsky's ideas, and to remind ourselves of children's abilities to write prior to or concurrently with learning to read. This is especially important to note given the preponderance of literacy programs and models for young children that emphasize reading first, and more reading than writing in the literacy ratio.

Glenda Bissex

Glenda Bissex's (1980) *GNYS AT WRK* remains, 30 years later, a groundbreaking account of her son Paul's writing and reading development from age 5 to 11. Working from the perspective of reading and writing as "abstractions" (p. ix) and that individuals read with a purpose, Bissex details Paul's discoveries, problem-solving strategies, and developmental attempts to make sense of literacy and make himself understood through writing. Following Read and Chomsky's work on early spelling, Bissex focuses on Paul's "invented spelling" as a window into his thinking and playing with sounds, letters, and words over time. She carefully documents his writing, as in an example from a day's writing of a book (one phrase per page for a total of 4 pages) when Paul was 5.1:

PAULS FAN
PAULS BAT
PAULS DP (DUMP)
PAULS GAMP ROP (JUMP ROPE) (p. 8)

Bissex shows how Paul's sound-symbol and writing journey is essentially one of problem-solving and playing with sounds, letters, and words to make important discoveries about writing. At age 5.6, Paul wrote 5 pages with a sentence per page:

WANS APNA TMTAR (Once upon a time there)
WAN SA BAR (wa- s a bear)
AD THTB AR WAT (and that bear went)
AWA AD E NAV (away and he nev-)
RKA MBK AGAN (er ca- me back again.)

Bissex comments on this moment in the evolution of Paul's writing:

> . . . Paul had moved from a semisyllabic writing system based on letter names as well as sounds to an alphabetic system in which finer sound distinctions were represented. Historically, this has also been the development of writing systems; the phonetic principle was expressed first through syllabic scripts and later through alphabetic scripts. (p. 24)

Paul's "struggle to work out an adequate representational system" (p. 31) for his spelling helped move him along the continuum of spelling insights toward conventional sound-symbol correspondence and spelling patterns. Later on, Paul moved away from this early "period of fluid invented spelling" to a greater "concern" for "correctness" and how to spell words and "whether a word was 'spelled right'" (p. 31). So Bissex's close analysis of Paul's spelling development helps us see, 30 years later, how much "developmental time" children need to play with sounds and letters as they move forward with increased accuracy and speed toward conventional spellings.

ATTENTION TO DEVELOPMENT

Starting in the 1970s, a strand of research looked at children's developmental capabilities in learning to write. The best-known pioneers in this area are Emilia Ferreiro of Mexico, Ana Teberosky of Spain, and Marie Clay of New Zealand.

Emilia Ferreiro and Ana Teberosky

Emilia Ferreiro and Anna Teberosky (1982) were interested in children's early reading and writing (in Spanish) from a Piagetian perspective. They were especially interested in how and why young children interpret their writing, and the evolution of children's writing as part of their overall cognitive development.

Ferreiro and Teberosky found five levels that indicate children's growth in writing. At Level 1, children make concrete connections between objects and words. For example, a child says that "writing" (actually strings of cursive lines) the word *bear* will be a longer word than writing the word *duck* since a bear is larger than a duck. Children at this level also do not differentiate between drawing and writing. At Level 2, children are more able to represent graphically conventional letters, although the total number of these graphic representations is still low. So children make do by varying the position of the letters within groupings. Children at this level also see that "each letter counts as part of the whole but has no worth in itself" (p. 192). For example, in their names, children understand that each letter has a place as part of their name, but they do not see each letter as a separate entity.

Children make a leap at Level 3 as they make an "attempt at assigning a sound value to each of the letters that compose a piece of writing" (p. 197). Children also see that "each letter stands for one syllable" (p. 197), and move away from a more "global" understanding of language and writing and toward a part to whole understanding of the constituent parts of words. At Level 4, children make discoveries that move them from the syllabic understanding of writing to the beginning of seeing writing as based on an alphabetic code. The child "abandons the syllabic hypothesis and discovers the need for an analysis that goes beyond the syllable . . ." (p. 204) and the realization that a minimum number of letters can now suffice to represent some words. At Level 5, the child more completely and fully understands writing as based on an alphabetic system. "In reaching this level, children have broken the code; they understand that each written character corresponds to a sound value smaller than a syllable, and they systematically analyze the phonemes of the words they are writing" (p. 209). Ferreiro and Teberosky also note that children may still have difficulty spelling conventionally, but that this does not indicate a general "writing problem" but only challenges "confined to orthography" (p. 209).

More recently, Ferreiro (2003) has looked at how we have too often collapsed varied literacy approaches into one all-encompassing framework. She argues, instead, for a view of literacy learning as more diverse and differentiated. Ferreiro believes that powerful literacy learning occurs when students:

1. interact with varied texts
2. have access to different social structures for reading and writing
3. experience varied forms and functions of written language
4. balance content and mechanics (ranging from "problems with graphic representation" to "textual organization")
5. take varied perspectives toward texts ("author, proofreader, commentator, evaluator, actor, etc.")
6. read and write between-the-lines in varied kinds of texts (p. 72)

These are the core elements for rich literacy teaching that can reach the varied talents and needs of contemporary students.

Marie Clay

Marie Clay (1975, 1998, 2005) has long been interested in children's developmental capabilities for learning to write, and in sharpening the theoretical and practical connections between oral language, reading, and writing. In her early work, Clay (1975) examined children's "gradual development of a perceptual awareness of those arbitrary customs" (p. 2) about print. Clay believed that children who engage in "creative writing" are "manipulating the units of written language—letters, words, sentence types" and are gaining "some awareness of how these can be combined to convey unspoken messages" (p. 2).

Clay looked at how six principles undergird children's early attempts to write and draw. These principles are the vehicle for children's efforts to make "gross approximations" (p. 15) about spelling and spatiality, and are "specific" to children's small insights about the forms and functions of writing. Clay also argues that children's early knowledge about writing can be so specific that one new insight or discovery can change "the child's perception of the entire system drastically, or may even disorganize it" (p. 15). As children begin to write, "there is so little system [i.e., writing knowledge and structure] and so much that is new" (p. 15).

Clay's principles are called Recurring, Directional, Generating, Inventory, Contrastive, and Abbreviation. The Recurring Principle is seen in children's drawings when children draw one object repeatedly, and in their writing when children know "only a few letters or words" and "take a short cut to a long statement by repeating the same symbol again and again and again" (p. 21). In the Directional Principle, children use letters and made-up signs to indicate "correct directional behavior" including "a top-left starting position," "movement from left to right," and a "return sweep" back to the "left-hand position under the starting point to establish the top to bottom progression" (p. 23).

In the Generating Principle, children combine and arrange letters, words, and symbols in different patterns to make longer strings. The Inventory Principle involves children writing down all the letters and/or words, an activity that "has value for the child in systematising those items which he can recall and which have become part of *his* written repertoire" (p. 31). In the Contrastive Principle, lines and letters are arranged in contrastive arrangements as children "create contrasts in visual form, letters, meaning, and sounds" (p. 37). The Abbreviation Principle is the "deliberate attempt to use one symbol, implying a full word, which the child could fill out or get help in filling out if he were asked to" (p. 38). For example, a child wrote "SOS" above a ship on the water.

Clay (1998, 2005) is also interested in developmental connnections between writing and reading.

> Most people find it difficult to think of writing and reading as two different ways of learning about the same thing—written language. It is like having two hands. (If you have ever had one hand out of action you will understand this metaphor.) What you know in writing can be helpul in your reading and vice versa, just as the right hand can help the left hand with holding or vice versa. (p. 22)

Clay (1998) sees four main effects on reading from an emphasis on writing. First, writing promotes a slower analysis or reflection on written language, which provides "the young learner with time and opportunity to observe visual things about printed language" (p. 138). Second, writing highlights letter forms, sequences, and clusters. Writing thus encourages children to "see letters and letter order within words" (p. 138). Third, writing encourages children to manipulate and build layers and levels of language involving "texts, sentences, phrases, words, sounds" (p. 138). Fourth, writing elevates children's reflection and awareness of language, to "bounce one kind of knowing off the other—to link, compare, contrast, and self-correct" (p. 139). Taken together, these elements promote "independent learners whose reading and writing improve whenever they read and write" (Clay, 2005, p. 22).

WRITING AS A PROCESS

Starting in the mid to late 1970s and 1980s, a number of American researchers and teachers looked closely at composing in the primary grades (Atwell, 1987; Calkins, 1986; Graves, 1983). These theorists and teachers formulated a set of pedagogical techniques around the central notion of writing as a process. This view was partially in response to the then current view of writing as product-based and based on teacher-selected topics and formats.

Donald Graves

Graves and other writing process adherents gained theoretical and empirical support from earlier work discussed above on young children's understanding of orthography and perceptions of print (Chomsky, 1971; Clay, 1975; Read, 1970). This line of research assisted process writing proponents in four critical ways:

1. uncovering more about children's writing abilities and links to oral language resources
2. relying on close observations and detailed analyses of children's written products
3. connecting early literacy research and theory with children's writing behaviors
4. proposing a view of children as active learners in their own literacy development

Graves (1983) saw the need for changes in how we conceptualize and teach writing, as well as changes to the basic ways that we approach the construction of knowledge and student-teacher and student-student relationships in classrooms. Graves advocated for writing as a "craft" and an artistic endeavor that emphasized "real and authentic" communication as teachers and students talk with each other before, during, and after writing. He emphasized the value of children doing what "real writers" do: brainstorming ideas, writing on a daily basis, writing multiple drafts of one piece, not overly worrying about spelling and punctuation in early drafts, conferencing with peers and adults, writing for a real audience, editing and revising, and then finally producing a "published" piece to be shared with peers and adults.

In this framework, children are encouraged to utilize their own lives and interests as the raw materials for learning to write. They choose their own topics and follow their own interests. Children's peers also play important roles, commenting on successive drafts of a piece of writing and providing audience responses as individual readers and in small and whole response groups. Children learn to help each other by:

1. increasing their awareness of what helps their writing
2. increasing their awareness of their current knowledge about their writing
3. learning to use new helping roles from peers
4. increasing access to each other (Graves, 1983, p. 37)

Graves called for an emphasis on "group consciousness" and for calling children's "attention to the way they listened to each other" (p. 39).

In this model, teachers also have new roles and expectations. Teachers function more as guides and mediators than as authoritative sources of knowledge and as transmitters of basic writing skills. Graves also emphasized the value of teachers writing on their own and writing alongside their students.

> The better the writer, the less the struggle. We maintain their fictions by not writing ourselves. Worse, we lose out on one of the most valuable ways to teach the craft. If they see us write, they will see the middle of the process, the hidden ground—from the choice of the topic to the final completion of the work. (p. 43)

Graves's "fictions" refer to students' beliefs that writing "flows" for adults and that it is easy for us. So if we write with and alongside children, they will see and hear that we, too, are learners and also struggle in our writing. When teachers write, it "makes explicit what children ordinarily can't see: how words go down on paper, and the thoughts that go with the decisions made in the writing" (p. 45).

Lucy Calkins

Calkins (2003, 2006) has recently expanded and consolidated her early work on writing as a process into a curriculum framework called "Units of Study." Calkins has co-written several books with colleagues from The Teachers College Reading and Writing Project that focus on grades K–2 and 3–5. The mostly month-long units of study focus on particular aspects of teaching writing and present theory and practice based upon Calkins's and others' work on the writing process approach. Student choice of writing topics, teacher mini-lessons, revision and multiple drafts, publishing, audience, sharing, and teachers writing—all hallmarks of the writing process approach—have prominent places in the units of study.

The K–2 units of study include a focus on conferencing with students, personal writing, poetry, revision, and nonfiction. The units are based on "cultivating rich conversations, lots of storytelling, and detailed drawings" (Calkins, 2003, *Launching the Writing Workshop*, p. 1). They are also based on classrooms that emphasize daily read-alouds, phonics and spelling, and "building" and "taking apart" words (Calkins, 2003, *The Nuts and Bolts of Teaching Writing*, p. 4).

The grade 3–5 units of study (Calkins, 2006) include a more in-depth writing workshop, personal narratives, persuasive essays, fiction, informational writing, and poetry. In this expanded writing workshop structure, teachers "look for teachable moments in which they can extend what children do as writers" and, at the start of the year, "scaffold a class of children to progress through a version of the writing process in a roughly synchronized fashion" (p. 13). Calkins also emphasizes that the curriculum focuses on "structure" and "process," and believes that "young writers would profit from learning to approach a draft with a specific text structure in mind" (p. 24).

SOCIOCULTURAL PERSPECTIVES

In this section, I highlight the work of Lisa Delpit and Anne Haas Dyson. These researchers have looked closely at the social, cultural, and linguistic roots and influences on children's literacy development.

Lisa Delpit

Delpit's (1986, 1988, 1998, 2002) early work looked critically at the value of process writing for African-American and other children of color who have historically received a marginalized education.

> Although the problem is not necessarily inherent in the method, in some instances adherents of the process approaches to writing create situations in which students ultimately find themselves held accountable for knowing a set of rules about which no one has ever directly informed them. Teachers do students no service to suggest, even implicitly, that "product" is not important. In this country, students will be judged on their product regardless of the process they utilized to achieve it. And that product, based as it is on the specific codes of a particular culture, is more readily produced when the directives of how to produce it are made explicit. (1988, p. 188)

Delpit argues that "to deny students their own expert knowledge is to disempower them" (p. 189). She advocates for students to gain "expert knowledge" involving the forms and conventions of written language, and not necessarily only children's own personal experiences and stories.

Delpit (1988) argues for more explicit and "direct" attention to written language forms and products, though she adds the caveat that ". . . merely adopting direct instruction is not the answer" (p. 189) and instead favors the dual approach outlined by Cazden (1988):

1. Continuous opportunities for writers to participate in some authentic bit of the unending conversation . . . thereby becoming part of a vital community of talkers and writers in a particular domain, and
2. Periodic, temporary focus on conventions of form, taught as cultural conventions expected in a particular community. (Delpit, 1988, p. 295)

Delpit, however, makes a distinction between the "domain" of literate/social activity and the acquisition of written forms, arguing that these two notions do not go hand in hand for *all* children.

Delpit (1998) also proposed that a cultural match between students and the literate ways of classrooms is not as important as teachers learning "how to recognize when there is a problem for a particular child and seek its cause in the most broadly conceived fashion" (Delpit, 1992, p. 237). Delpit (1992) identifies a "cultural clash" between home and school that is actualized in two ways: 1. teachers misread students' abilities and talents and 2. "teachers utilize styles of instruction and/or discipline that are at odds with community norms" (p. 238). These difficulties relate to an "underlying attitudinal difference in the appropriate display of explicitness and personal power in the classroom" (p. 239).

In terms of literacy instruction, Delpit argues that skills-based approaches teach "less" by "focusing solely on isolated, decontextualized bits" of language (p. 242). Delpit argues that teachers who favor a writing process approach and "are unfamiliar with the language abilities of African American children are led to believe that these students have no fluency with language" (p. 243). This can result in children remaining mired in the early stages of multiple drafting, and being denied opportunities to advance to more complex and higher-level stages in process pedagogy. Again, "the key here is not the kind of instruction but the attitude underlying it" (p. 243), and the work of teachers to understand and support children's language and literacy needs.

Anne Haas Dyson

Dyson (1986, 1989, 1993, 2003) is interested in expanding our conception of how children learn to write beyond a monolithic view of one path fits all. She focuses on the varied and diverse ways that children become symbol users and symbol weavers, and how powerful writing relies on oral

language, social interaction, and children's sociocultural talents and traditions. Drawing on the work of Vygotsky and Bakhtin among others, Dyson
argues that there is an ongoing and dynamic interplay between multiple
worlds, what happens off the page is as important as what happens on it—
talk and social interaction in and around literacy events are embedded in the
ongoing social relationships of all the participants in classroom life. Literacy
and language use are part and parcel of the ways children and adults learn
about each other, themselves, and the worlds they live in. For Dyson (1989),
"each child's symbolizing" is "an expression of that child and shaped by
that child's ongoing experiences in school and by her or his reflections on
the wider world" (p. 255).

Children are active symbol users and manipulators of the boundaries or
the tensions (such as time and space considerations in creating stories and
other kinds of writing) between a variety of forms and functions of talk,
drawing, and writing as well as social relationships. Children also draw on
their own individual styles and resources to manipulate a range of symbolic
and "real" worlds—the world represented on the drawn and written page,
the world of the imagination, the immediate social world of the classroom,
and the larger experienced world outside. Along the way, children's writing
becomes a more embedded and dynamic part of the ongoing social life and
intellectual community in the classroom.

Children's writing is influenced by the "official world" of the classroom, as well as the "unofficial world" of their peers (Dyson & Genishi,
2009). And when teachers open up their classrooms to the range of children's linguistic, social, and cultural talents and interests, this helps go beyond a "narrow range of social and textual experiences" (Dyson, 2003,
p. 212) for children. Dyson (2000) argues that we can support chidren's
"sea of voices" for literacy by providing "time and ideological space (for
instance, different perspectives or orientations to subject matter) and the
support of at least some familiar social waters (such as events)" (p. 60).

LITERACY AND NEW LANGUAGE LEARNERS

This section presents ideas from María de la Luz Reyes, Katharine Samway,
and Eve Gregory on effective literacy education for new language learners.

María de la Luz Reyes

María de la Luz Reyes (1992) is concerned about how well writing instruction, and the process approach in particular, supports new language learners. Reyes argues that some students in process writing classrooms receive

covert and overt messages that English is to supercede the use of other languages in writing. The effect is that this "offers teachers no compelling reason to change their teaching strategies to meet the needs of linguistically diverse students. . . ." (p. 433) Reyes also argues that "it does not mean that students should not learn to speak, read, and write English well . . .", but that English should not "supplant" native languages" (p. 435). Reyes advocates against "a one size fits all" approach to writing, and for teachers to implement aspects of process writing with "modifications" (p. 435) for new language learners. By linking a view of education and writing instruction as both emphasizing the process of learning, in an overall way Reyes cautions us that "even otherwise good teachers can be unsure about when to let the process take its natural course, and when to mediate instruction" (p. 137). For Reyes, "cultural and linguistic factors" are critical for pedagogy and for writing instruction, and we must remember not to "relinquish" our roles "as mediators of knowledge" and to remember the "importance of form" (p. 443).

Katharine Samway

Samway (2006) has looked at the linguistic talents and needs of new language learners learning to write. Samway argues that young writers learning English are "capable of expressing complex thoughts, even if they do not have control of the English writing system" (p. 30). New language learners can "understand more than they are able to express in writing" (p. 34), and so it is critical that we provide sufficiently challenging and high-level writing tasks and projects. To express and communicate their complex thoughts and ideas, new language learners often rely on printed matter, visuals, and symbols in their environment. New language learners also move through certain developmental stages in writing (from scribble writing to letters representing whole words to standardized writing) and face challenges integrating content and mechanics similar to those faced by other young writers.

For instance, Samway cites the work of Heald-Taylor (1986), who studied the writing of Linh, a 1st-grader who worked to find an equilibrium between content and mechanics:

> Linh had begun to focus more on the content of her writing and by the end of the month was no longer using scribble to act as a place holder for unknown spellings of words or parts of words. This increased focus on the content of her writing continued . . . [until a year later] her writing integrated attention to conventions, as well as content. (Samway, 2006, p. 43)

Linh and other new language learners' use of "place holders" is one of many strategies they use to problem-solve patterns and conventions in a new language. Samway points out that the writing progress of Linh and other new language learners indicates "what they are capable of doing" when we "expect them to do complex cognitive and linguistic tasks" even though we might think "that they don't have enough English" (p. 52).

Eve Gregory

Gregory (2001, 2008) has focused on the talents and needs of new language learners, and is particularly interested in home-school connections and children's community-based ways of using, understanding, and producing literacy. Gregory (2008) uses the term *new language learners*, which I adopt throughout this book.

> [A new language learner] is a child who is at an early stage or who still lacks fluency in a second or additional language but whose ultimate aim is to become as fluent as possible, that is, able to communicate easily with others in the language and able positively to identify with both (or all if more than two are being learned) language groups and cultures. (p. 1)

Gregory (2001) argues that children's "cultural knowledge" is influenced by experiences with literacy in homes and communities, and through the particular socially and cognitively based strategies that children and adults engage in together. For example, in looking at children's play and literacy use in "informal" learning situations such as in children's homes and communities, Gregory (2001) looks "beyond existing metaphors of 'scaffolding,' 'guided participation' or 'collaborative learning' to explain the reciprocity that might be taking place between young siblings" (p. 305). Gregory emphasizes the power of "synergy, a unique reciprocity whereby siblings act as adjuvants in each other's learning" (p. 309), and older children teach younger children and thereby increase their own literacy learning. In this process of synergy, siblings engage in "cultural routines" around literacy that provide a complex and influential set of interactions using oral and nonverbal language.

Gregory (2008) is also interested in the interrelationships between cultures, codes, and contexts in the literacy learning of new language learners. Borrowing on Vygotskian and other sociocultural perspectives, Gregory emphasizes the theoretical and practical power of two frameworks: the inside-out and the outside-in approaches. In the inside-out approach, literacy instruction "starts from the child's own knowledge and experience and gradually moves outwards into the new world; it starts from the smallest units of meaning, the letters and words, and gradually links these into complete texts" (p. 160). Gregory notes that the inside-out approach is not only based on children's known experiences, but includes the range of new and future literacy experiences and knowledge that are to come.

The outside-in approach utilizes stories and narrative. It emphasizes story stucture, story language, chunking of story language, sociomoral aspects of stories, and semantic, syntactic, bibliographic, lexical, and graphophonic literacy clues (p. 184). The outside-in approach also offers new language learners "the process of initiation into a new culture" (p 186), and this process becomes even "more meaningful" through "first-hand experiences" with literacy and other activities. Gregory argues for the ultimate goal of integrating the inside-out and outside-in approaches to literacy to promote rich and long-lasting learning for new language learners.

This chapter has provided an overview, in mostly historical and chronological form, of key theorists' ideas and strategies for promoting powerful literacy learning for children. The chapter is, of course, not exhaustive, but it provides a useful theoretical and pedagogical background for looking more closely at integrating written language mechanics and content in the book's remaining chapters.

Chapter 2

CONTENT AND MECHANICS

Daniel: What's hard and easy about writing?

Vanessa (kindergartner): It's really easy. You can know the words—what sounds they make. Mo Willems books are easy to read. They make you learn a lot and read—we copy the books so we can make the pigeon pictures.

Rickey (kindergartner): Drawing a scorpion, make a picture and write—the teacher don't be there for us every time. She has stuff to do, attendance and other kids.

When I first envisioned this book, and then began talking with classroom teachers, I looked for a clear demarcation between definitions of "content and meaning" and "mechanics or conventions" in written language instruction. What I found, though, is somewhat different. I found that the idea and the definition of content and mechanics are more tied to one's philosophy of education and one's view of teaching and learning. I also found that the teachers with whom I spoke were a bit surprised at my question of how to define content and mechanics, and how they approached the integration of the two. While this appeared to be a somewhat novel question for them, it also appeared that they did not think about these two elements as separate. Although I was relieved and heartened that they thought of them as integrated and combined, for this is what this book is all about, I also tried to understand how they viewed the two elements and how they broke them down in their teaching mind and in their actual writing instruction. Before I present each teacher's views on writing content and mechanics, I provide a brief description of her classroom and school context. I also emphasize here that all of the teachers teach in schools and districts with a moderate amount of freedom to envision and teach literacy and writing as they see fit.

WHAT'S BASIC ABOUT WRITING WELL?

Skills

Forty years ago, the English researchers Nancy Martin and Jeremy Mulford (1971) pointed out that "'skill' has the attraction for a teacher of seeming to be something which can not only be objectively defined but also exists in its own right and *therefore* be passed on as a sort of entity" (p. 153). In the Introduction to this book, I discussed how writing mechanics are often depicted as more tangible and easy to see and identify than content, and thus are more likely to be emphasized in writing objectives, standards, assessments, and therefore, teaching.

Twenty years ago, James Moffett (1988) argued for a broader view of what constitutes writing, and pointed out that schools as institutions are directed by literacy policy to teach writing in certain ways. In the cause of "institutional convenience (usually beyond the control of teachers themselves)," writing is pushed down toward lower levels of writing excellence and originality in the name of putting the "institution over the individual" and "form over content" (p. 74). This dynamic leads to a "superficial view that spelling and punctuating are basic skills" instead of "thinking and speaking," and also to an "analytic isolation of language units as curriculum units (the phoneme, the word, the sentence, the paragraph)" (p. 75). What we mean by "basic" and by "skill" in writing instruction theory and practice, then, is linked to a range of influences of which we may not be fully in control.

Standards

For instance, although the California English–Language Arts Content Standards (California Department of Education, 1998) emphasize that "reading, writing, listening, and speaking are not disembodied skills" and exist "in context and in relation to the others" (p. vii), they are seen as "skills that invariably improve with study and practice" (p. vii). The grade-level standards delineate specific writing "strategies," "applications," and "conventions" to be taught and mastered. As children move up from kindergarten to grade 4, these elements include:

- organization and focus
- spelling
- penmanship
- sentence structure

- writing about books
- writing brief narratives
- writing brief expository descriptions
- grammar
- punctuation
- capitalization
- understanding purposes of various reference materials
- revising original drafts
- writing a friendly letter
- developing a topic sentence
- creating multiple-paragraph compositions
- keyboarding skills
- writing responses to literature
- writing information reports
- writing summaries

If we isolate only spelling, the following are sample expectations for spelling skills:

> *Kindergarten:* Spelling independently by using pre-phonetic knowl-
> edge, sounds of the alphabet, and knowledge of letter names
> *1st grade:* Spelling three- and four-letter short-vowel words and grade-
> level-appropriate sight words correctly.
> *2nd grade:* Spelling frequently used, irregular words correctly; spell
> basic short-vowel, r-controlled, and consonant-blend patterns
> correctly.
> *3rd grade:* Spelling correctly one-syllable words that have blends,
> contractions, compounds, orthographic patterns.
> *4th grade:* Spelling correctly roots, inflections, suffixes and prefixes,
> and syllable constructions.

But these standards and expectations do not add up to the whole story of teaching children to write well. For Liz Goss, a 2nd-grade teacher featured in this book, standards for writing content and mechanics at best give us "clues" about "what is 2nd-grade writing." Liz, as well as the other teachers presented in this book, gathers additional information and knowledge from multiple sources and continually adjusts and fine-tunes her expectations about what is reasonable to expect her students to write.

Martin and Mulford (1971), writing long before the recent proliferation of writing standards, also caution against the allure of conventions as the gold standard.

> But we would maintain that a child who observed all the conventions with perfect competence, yet whose writing was uniformly unengaged, should not be called a skilled writer—not even in a "basic" sense. Indeed, it would be precisely what is basic that was lacking in his writing behavior. We use, here, the phrase "writing behavior" in order to stress the activity of writing, the *process*, as against the *product*. (p. 153)

So the idea of "skills" and a "skilled writer" needs to go beyond a list of mastery of written language conventions.

> It is, in fact, difficult if not impossible to judge where to draw the line between usages that are conventional only for tidiness's sake and those that have a greater significance. It is probably more helpful to distinguish between those that have chiefly to do with what we shall call "presentation," and those that are intrinsic to the communication of meaning. (Martin & Mulford, 1971, p. 157)

As we continue to break down what we mean by "skills" *vis-à-vis* content and mechanics, we see that there are levels of complexity and value in terms of integrating content and mechanics. It is a new challenge, then, to look closely at those mechanics that are related to "presentation," and those that influence a deeper "communication of meaning." It is not that the conventions of presentation are not important; they are, but there is much more to the journey of learning to write well than mastery of a finite set of mechanics.

> The business of helping children directly with their writing is a difficult one. They readily interpret instruction as the learning of rules, and we suggest that the basic matter of writing about what concerns you is not readily susceptible to rules; this is the reason that we make a distinction between skilled writing behavior and the learning of surface competences. (Martin & Mulford, 1971, p. 161)

When we look at ways to integrate content and mechanics, it is helpful conceptually and pedagogically to distinguish between deep content/mechanics integration ("skilled writing behavior") and mastery of isolated mechanics that don't alone add up to powerful writing ("learning of surface competences").

Children's Perspectives

Although little researched or understood, young writers have their own views regarding what it means to write well. Stacia Stribling and Susan Kraus (2007), a university-based teacher educator and a first-grade teacher, respectively, wanted to find ways to help their students focus more on content in their writing. They asked their 1st-grade students for their opinions on what makes for "good writing," and their students "overwhelmingly agreed that you could tell that something is well written by how it looks . . . by neat handwriting, capitals, periods, and other mechanical conventions" (p. 6). When asked, "What's the most important thing a writer needs to remember?," student responses, which Stribling and Straus surmised were primarily influenced by adult definition of writing, included:

- How to spell
- First, a period—then after that you need an uppercase, and then a period at the end
- Mostly to remember how to make sure that he doesn't make too many mistakes . . . to make sure his letters aren't floating—that's the most important thing
- To write the letters corrrect where the left and right; the 'd' goes one way and the 'b' goes the other way.

But when the children were asked to comment on their own writing, their responses changed. The children "focused on content . . . what it does for them aesthetically, how it makes them feel, how creative they were" (p. 6). Stribling and Kraus note that content motivates students to write, but that they are still preoccupied with proper conventions. Even when they tried to focus more on content, Stribling and Kraus found themselves "commenting on the way their [students'] writing looked—whether it had proper punctuation and capitalization" (p. 8). "Torn between celebrating children's passion for writing compelling stories and worrying about their inability to consistently use proper mechanics" (p. 13), Stribling and Kraus resolved to find new ways to integrate content and mechanics as they ultimately realized that "it is impossible to think that we can have all of the pieces (content and mechanics) in place all the time" (p. 15).

CONSTRUCTING KNOWLEDGE

Definitions of and strategies for teaching written language content and mechanics are now largely dictated by state content standards. Yet, the fostering of accurate and inventive long-term writing knowledge and talent comes about through the philosophies, ideas, and strategies of individual and groups of teachers thinking, teaching, and reflecting on their own teaching. A helpful first step is to see that writing standards, whether for content or for mechanics, do provide helpful signposts along the long journey of learning to write well. The next step involves defining for ourselves how we see content and mechanics fitting into what it means to write well and how we integrate content and mechanics. This is the step that this chapter focuses on.

Where do we start, and what do we go on? If we believe in constructivist learning theories, and that children learn through discovery and expert guidance, then what does this mean for integrating written language content and mechanics? I once heard a teacher talk about constructivist education and the idea of having students construct their own learning and knowledge. The teacher then stated that if students don't have the necessary raw materials—ideas, experiences, skills, information, resources, tools—then students need to be provided and supported with these elements before they can construct any new learning and knowledge. They can't simply pull it out of thin air. Applying her comments to writing instruction, we need to remember that over-attention to meaning and content *at the expense* of written language conventions means we are asking young writers to construct without the necessary building materials.

A key challenge, then, is for us to revisit how we conceptualize and teach content and mechanics integration. As one anonymous reviewer of the proposal for this book argued, we need "to see the importance of using conventions in the service of making meaning through writing, rather than practicing the conventions in and of themselves." This is important for all children, and is especially critical for new language learners (Gregory, 2008), who are learning additional languages. New language learners benefit from specific and sustained support in identifying, using, and reflecting on the raw materials of written language forms and structures in both their home language and the new target language.

The seven exemplary teachers with whom I spoke all formulated their own definitions of mechanics and content, and expressed their ideas on ways that they integrated the two in their writing philosophy, curriculum, and teaching. I have arranged their definitions of mechanics and content by grade level to show grade-level-specific ideas, and how the teachers' views fit developmental expectations for students at particular grades. Since the teachers have all taught multiple grade levels, their definitions and perspectives also speak to their cross-grade-level experience.

Kindergarten: "Starting With Content"

Florence Tse, an English/Chinese bilingual speaker, teaches kindergarten and her most recent class is composed of 15 mostly first-generation Chinese-American children who speak Chinese at home. The other five children are also new language learners who speak various other languages. Florence's classroom is an ELD classroom and she uses her Chinese on an informal basis to support her children's literacy understanding as needed.

Florence starts her school year with "interactive drawings" and a lot of support for children's literacy engagement, so their earliest writing experiences are not heavily dependent on English oral language proficiency.

> We talk a lot about how to look at our classmates and observe carefully and focus on drawings rather than writing, which really stems from just putting print on paper and so the idea is that we're looking at our friends closely. I model and we draw the pictures together. Then we add writing. We basically clap how many words they want to use in their sentence to express their thought, and whatever words they do know how to write, we write it, and whatever they don't, they just put a blank there. So there's really no pressure in terms of having to spell out that word.

Florence emphasizes the power of pictures and drawings as a form of writing (Vygotsky, 1978, 1986), and provides a predictable format and strong support (Reyes, 1992; Samway, 2006) for her new language learners. Florence also takes an inside-out approach (Gregory, 2008), paying attention to small units of meaning, as she breaks down the writing challenge, helping children clap out the words in their sentence. This makes for a developmentally appropriate beginning to writing that supports her new language learners. Florence, in her teaching and writing mind, seeks an overall integration of content and mechanics, but follows a teaching sequence that begins with content.

> I start with content so that my students get their ideas out. Most of my students at the beginning of the school are pretty nonverbal in English, so it's very important for me to have their ideas stated. So content before mechanics. I see content as, what's important? What's your point? Why are we writing this? We always have to be very explicit about our objectives in our writing—we're writing for a purpose.

Although her students have few resources for producing oral and written English, Florence emphasizes content over mechanics to give her students' content and ideas a preeminent position as the children start their writing journey.

Later in the fall, and then over the course of the school year, Florence adds increased attention to mechanics.

I talk about capitalization, spacing between words, correct grammar, figuring out if the sentence was about the past, the present, or something that's happening later on in the future. I also have the students reread what they're writing, and ask themselves, "Does this make sense?"

By breaking down elements of written conventions, and also paying attention to meaning and content, Florence integrates the two over the course of the kindergarten year.

First Grade: "To Have Their Own Ideas"

Ilsa Miller has taught kindergarten, 1st grade, a combined kindergarten/ grade 1, and 3rd grade. She currently teaches at an independent school in San Francisco, and her classes average 22 students. Her students are 66% Anglo-European descent and 34% children of color and all are monolingual English speakers who mostly read and write at 1st-grade level and above.

When I think of mechanics, I think of conventions: syntax, sentence structure, capitals, periods, word choice, editing, and spelling at a level that can be reread by the student author.

Ilsa expands on the conventions noted by Florence for kindergarten, and adds other elements such as word choice, editing, and reading back one's own written text.

Mechanics is also about the editing process. We do a lot of peer editing to introduce and bring awareness to the editing process, which seems to help 1st-graders look at their own work more critically. Rather than just saying, "I'm done," they understand what I mean when I ask them to reread their writing and edit for specific conventions and revise.

Teaching 1st-graders, who are more capable developmentally than kindergartners to work together and reflect on their writing, Ilsa sees mechanics as taking on more sophisticated elements in a connected way.

Ilsa also sees crossover for 1st-graders between content and mechanics.

Word choice is part mechanics, and also part content. It's often a matter of the "what" and the "how" for children in having to pay attention to content and mechanics. For instance, when children improve a sentence by revising certain words, they do so in a content-specific way.

As befits the cognitive and linguistic capabilities of 1st-graders, Ilsa sees 1st-graders juggling the "what" and the "how" of writing as they learn to connect the two elements. This harkens back to the work of Ferreiro and Teberosky (1982), who looked at advances in children's writing as children gained new cognitive insights into the forms and functions of written language.

Ilsa also sees content and mechanics integration as linked to the issue of "correctness," which is connected to the discussion of "basic skills" earlier in this chapter. Ilsa encourages her students to develop their own healthy internal balance between how content and mechanics connect.

> I want each writer and their peers to be able to read or listen to a piece of writing and get a sense of the story or poem without getting stuck on conventions. But that doesn't mean that all the conventions are correct. In fact, it would be odd if they were because then the children would be spending too much time on mechanics and not enough on the content. If the mechanics were all correct at the level I teach, I would worry about that. Usually, when I see children who are paying more attention to mechanics than content, an element of story or some other kind of writing is missing in their piece.

Ilsa values the overall goal of keeping 5- and 6-year-olds involved and engaged in this integration act rather than an overemphasis on entirely correct mechanics.

Second Grade: "To Know the Expectations for Content and Mechanics"

Second grade begins a break from the K–1 span by extending the depth and breadth of expectations for children to integrate content and mechanics. It is the beginning of a surge in some children's writing in terms of the length of written pieces, linguistic complexity, range of genres, mastery of mechanics, linking with informational and narrative texts, imitation of writers' styles, and incorporation of literary and poetic devices.

Liz Goss teaches at Legacy Charter School on the West Side of Chicago. She has taught kindergarten, 1st grade, and 2nd grade for 9 years. Her current class of 26 students are of African-American descent, and about 30% of her students enter her 2nd-grade class reading and writing on grade level, with the remaining students reading and writing below grade level. Liz sees mechanics and content through the lens of her students' developmental and literacy talent and needs.

> Mechanics are what a mechanic does to be sure the car is functioning—it is not pretty or artful, and is more scientific and exact. There are choices in mechanics but there is not free rein. There are rules that have to be followed. They exist so the writing can "drive" and a reader can understand the meaning. Writing is a form of communication and if a reader cannot understand the writing, then the mechanics have to be addressed. For 2nd grade, I find that mechanics run the spectrum from finger spacing for a few students, to remembering and understanding punctuation (commas in a list, apostrophes to show ownership, periods, question marks, quotation marks) to learning about complete sentences and subject/verb agreement.

Liz's vision of mechanics is about the nuts and bolts that form the foundation for learning to write well. Liz also does not see mechanics as applied wholesale to a group of students, and instead emphasizes the value of matching particular mechanics to particular students. In the spirit of Vygotsky, Britton, Clay, and others, Liz's view of the place of mechanics in writing instruction is closely tied to where children are developmentally and where they need to go with her support and that of peers.

Liz sees content as the essence of writing well. Content "includes ideas, word choice, and genre. It is the heart of the writing, as well as some of the craft and art." Liz also recognizes how her view of integrating content and mechanics has changed as she has evolved as a teacher.

> At the beginning of my teaching career I focused mostly on content. I wanted students engaged in what they were writing. I stressed writing as a way to understand the world and to communicate that understanding. I focused on some basic mechanics (finger spacing, end marks) but mostly I wanted students to be *writers*—people who *had* to write because that is what they do, like breathe or skip. I wanted them to own the title "author." I emphasize the power of becoming fluent with different genres, understanding how each genre fits each author differently. This is one of my favorite experiences each year: watching each child discover which genres fit for them. Some come to 2nd grade knowing they love to write or they hate to write. It is my mission that by the end of the year they know which type of writing they *love*. There are always a few reluctant writers—the most verbal ones about this are the boys. But I convince them that if they stick with me they will love some types of writing. My main goal remains

helping all my students see themselves as authors, but I have become more adept at introducing and reinforcing mechanics along the way as part of the work of writers.

For Liz, children learn the tangibles (mechanics) of learning to write well through the discovery of the intangibles (content) of writing well and "falling in love with particular kinds of writing." Liz keeps in mind the developmental parameters of her students, and how "difficult it can be for 7- and 8-year-olds to focus on both content and mechanics at the same time when they write. I have seen students so excited about an idea, that they write four pages without one punctuated sentence."

Amanda Abarbanel-Rice teaches 2nd grade at Thousand Oaks Elementary School in Berkeley, California. Her current class of 20 students is almost evenly divided between African-American, Latina/o, Anglo-European, and children of mixed ancestry. In terms of literacy development, approximately one-third of her class enters on grade level, one-third at least one grade above, and one-third below grade level.

Amanda sees content and mechanics as integrated and hard to separate out in her teaching mind and view of what it means to write well.

At this point in my career of teaching writing, I see content and mechanics as very much integrated. Sometimes, as in poetry and other genres, mechanics can actually inform the content. But in general, I find that isolated mechanics lessons, which I do teach and are necessary, should be done in moderation. I believe in teaching a culture of mechanics, which is the expectation that students are always thinking about mechanics. Especially in 2nd grade, and also in the lower grades if I were teach them again, I'd emphasize a habit of mind and a practice habit, which is whenever you write something, you reread it. You're always making sure that it's making sense and that you are saying what you want to say.

Amanda emphasizes a "habit of mind" and a "habit of practice" that integrate content and mechanics in her philosophy of teaching writing and her teaching practices.

Amanda sees several main areas of mechanics for 2nd grade.

Mechanics in 2nd grade include punctuation, starting sentences with capital letters, and spelling. For some children, it's also spaces between words. These are primarily the front and center mechanics for this age group. Of course, there are other mechanics in writing, but these are

> most central. And I also relate mechanics in writing with reading. For example, later in the year, we read and write nonfiction pieces, and when we read certain texts, I point out certain elements of mechanics or structure in the nonfiction texts that include pictures, photos and captions, table of contents, index, glossary, diagrams, and charts.

These elements are embedded and focused on in Amanda's writer's workshop mini-lessons (Calkins, 2003), her writing conferences, and the children's peer editing.

> The habit of mechanics is for students to observe and monitor their own mechanics before, during, and after they write. Most importantly, as children get to be better writers, they pay attention to mechanics *as* they are writing. The overall goal is for writers to go back and forth between content and mechanics. For instance, when I am writing, I can be really focused on the content and then go back later and do more mechanics. It really depends on what the content is, and it's a similar process for children.

Amanda's view of content and mechanics integration echoes Stephen Sondheim's comment that he goes back and forth between focusing on writing music and writing the lyrics or words in his musicals. Second-graders are at a developmental point where they can begin focusing more on the integration *as* they are writing—a huge developmental leap from kindergarten and grade 1.

Grade 3: "Our Reading Has to Match Our Writing"

In 3rd grade, the idea of content and mechanics integration is even more strongly tied to reading across content areas, accessing varied texts, using varied levels of academic language, increasing vocabulary, extended revision and drafting of writing, and a sense of oneself as an author and writer.

Joli Gordon teaches 3rd grade at Clarendon Elementary School in San Francisco, and Madhuvanti Khare teaches 3rd grade at Berkeley Arts Magnet Elementary School in Berkeley. Their classes are similar in composition: Both total approximately 24 students comprised of 30% Anglo, 25% African-American, 25% Latina/o, and 20% of mixed ancestry, and approximately 30% are above grade level in literacy, 50% are at grade level, and 20% are below grade level. Both Joli and Madhuvanti see writing content and mechanics as deepening and broadening children's writing in the lower grades, and they especially emphasize the power of linking reading and writing for promoting an integration of content and mechanics.

Joli focuses on integration of content and mechanics as her students write about what they read in language arts and social studies, and focuses on isolated aspects of mechanics during her writer's workshop.

> The first half of the year focuses on story form, and I use a lot of stories to connect reading and writing. We do the reading first. We really get into a lot of different stories. We start off with silly stories, legends, and fairy tales. We do a lot of different genre studies, just getting into the reading and getting into the stories and characters, reading strategies, and then the writing content and mechanics piggyback on the reading. So, once the students are exposed to a lot of different stories, we reread them, but instead of reading like a reader, we read like a writer, which is an idea I got from the author of *Wondrous Words* (Ray, 1999). We look at what makes for a well-told story and transfer that certain aspect or strand into our writing. So we revisit the stories that we love so much, using them as mentor texts. Depending on where we are in the writing process, I also link content and mechanics wherever I can.

Joli sees the high-level integration of written language content and mechanics as coming about through the process of linking reading and writing (Calkins, 2006; Mermelstein, 2006). She also emphasizes mentor texts, which are key books or stories that serve as models for certain elements of teaching writing. They also facilitate discussion and the linking of elements in the mentor texts with elements in students' own writing.

Joli also bases her content and mechanics integration on the power of story (Dyson & Genishi, 1994; Gregory, 2008; Meier, 1988). Her emphasis on story and narrative echoes Eve Gregory's (2008) outside-in approach, where children learn to read and write through the forms and functions of stories. They learn critical elements of narrative—setting, plot, characterization, voice, narration, story language, and more—through the reading and discussion of varied texts and genres.

> Writing takes a lot of time. Because what do real writers do? They write all day. It takes them years to publish a book, so we can't expect children to publish a piece of writing in a week. So my reading matches my writing. That's why I spend a long time reading stories and also because entering 3rd-graders are more comfortable with story form from the earlier grades. They are more used to having stories read to them than information texts, and they're more familiar with the beginning, middle, and end structure of many stories.

Joli not only builds on her children's knowledge of story forms from the earlier grades, but sees that content and mechanics integration in writing must be matched with time devoted to reading, talking about, and reflecting on published texts. This echoes Marie Clay's (1998) idea that writing elevates children's reflection and awareness of language—to "bounce one kind of knowing off the other—to link, compare, contrast, and self-correct" (p. 139).

Joli also integrates content and mechanics through a year-long focus on social studies and science projects.

> Engaging content in writing comes from our content-related projects and activities. For example, we just finished a unit on the 1906 San Francisco earthquake and we watched videos and just got really excited reading and comparing primary sources. We had speakers come in and what really got us excited was, while we were watching this really great video on the earthquake and fire, the video mentioned a famous photographer who took photos during the fire with the last name of Monaco and one of my students said, "Hey, that's my last name, too," and we were all giggling because it was the same last name. Then suddenly the grandchild of the photographer came on the video and started talking about his grandfather's photos and my student said, "That's my grandfather." It turned out that J. B. Monaco was a famous photographer and he was my student's great-great-grandfather and he didn't know it. Of course, we got his grandfather to come in and he did a presentation. So content for writing comes about when we are learning about history or science, and we are learning about the structures and histories of events, doing inquiry, asking questions, and researching.

Joli also distinguishes between content and mechanics within her writing and content curriculum. She focuses more on mechanics in her writer's workshop mini-lessons (Calkins, 2006) and more on content when her students write in social studies and science.

> I don't assign any formal writing assignments connected with my social studies and science units. Instead, I assign quick-writes to help my students make connections and clarify their own thinking, as well as providing me with a quick assessment. Again, we reread texts connected with these units later when my students complete their own research project for writer's workshop. Instead, we do quick-writes to reflect, investigate, and question what we are learning in social studies

and science. I don't worry about the mechanics of writing for their quick-writes because that is not my objective. That's what we do in our writer's workshop, focus on mechanics through mini-lessons and also through peer editing and my own conferencing with individual children. We focus on content in their science journals, math journals, and sometimes in their writer's notebook, which is a place for my students to write down their writing ideas, raw material, and even draw pictures. For example, when we were studying the civil rights movement, before having discussions about something we read, listened to, or watched, I would first give my students 5 minutes to write out their thoughts on our discussion questions, and then they bring their writing to the rug for discussion.

So Joli, in her teaching mind, sees mechanics and content integration as occuring in different ways in selected aspects of her writing and content curriculum.

Madhuvanti Khare, another 3rd-grade teacher, also emphasizes attention to writing content through children's reading experiences, and writing mechanics through mini-lessons and peer and teacher editing. She sees mechanics as the nuts and bolts of writing.

Mechanics include punctuation, indenting for paragraphs, spelling, sentence variety, topic sentence, details, and main idea, though main idea crosses the line a little bit into content.

Madhuvanti, like Joli, emphasizes mechanics and content integration for 3rd-graders.

I focus on content in writing through the study of different genres. For example, poetry is one genre that we usually start the year with. When we're learning about haiku, the mechanics include knowing about how many syllables each line gets and knowing that it's a three-line poem and then the content involves thinking about how haiku generally refer to a season and emphasize nature.

Madhuvanti often starts with poetry and memoir/personal narrative because they emphasize content over mechanics, and also encourage a flexible disposition toward mechanics. This beginning also allows Madhuvanti to learn about her students as writers and as individuals.

Starting with poetry and personal narratives helps me get to know my students, what they like, what they dislike, what they're interested

> in. When you're meeting children for the first time, it's good to know stories about their families or their best vacation story because this writing helps me choose books for them to read, books for me to read to them, and also ideas for how to guide them in their writing.

By mixing poetry and personal narratives, Madhuvanti uses genres as the underlying structure to set the tone for emphasizing content and at the same time to break down elements of mechanics. Her poetry and personal narrative studies are followed by realistic fiction, fables, folktales and fairy tales, biography, and finally nonfiction. Each genre study lasts about 6–8 weeks.

Poetry has particular power for Madhuvanti to concretely show her 3rd-graders how to play with mechanics to influence content.

> The earlier you can start children with poetry the better, because they will have fewer inhibitions and feel really free. I talk with my students about how you don't have to be really strict with mechanics in poetry. I discuss mechanics such as punctuation and capitalization and show my students that the poetry of e.e. cummings often has no capital letters at all. I let them know that poets know the right way to punctuate in English and the right way to capitalize in English, but they don't necessarily feel bound by these conventions and that when they choose not to, it's for a reason. This insight gives students a kind of a power, too, in understanding why writers punctuate the way they do.

Madhuvanti starts first with a particular genre and then focuses on content and mechanics within the process of genre study, reading, writing, and discussion. In effect, Madhuvanti's approach integrates Eve Gregory's (2008) inside-out and outside-in approaches, where attention to the basic elements of written language such as words and sentences are melded with larger units such as stories, narratives, and other genres.

> I don't directly talk to my students about content and mechanics. Instead, we talk about topic or theme and I say, "What are we going to write our poems about? What is it going to be about?" That would be the content part and then for knowing how to break it down, we talk about syllables or lines and use poetry language—stanza, line breaks, rhyme, sequence. I usually spend about 75% of the time talking about what the poem is going to be about and about 25% addressing how students are going to make sure they have the right number of syllables and other elements of mechanics. I also point out content and mechanics through mentor texts. I have lots of poetry books that the children have free access to, and sometimes the children get a little

more hung up on the mechanics than poets do. I'll find them reading
and then really counting out the syllables to see if a poet followed the
rules or not.

Madhuvanti, like Joli, emphasizes the importance of transfer and connections between reading and writing. They both use mentor texts to highlight
certain elements of content and mechanics.

> Before we do any writing unit, we tend to do a lot of read-alouds of
> that genre. So as we're moving out of personal narrative, and while the
> children are still writing, I start reading in the next genre. The children
> publish their writing five or six times a year, and usually when the
> children are in the last week or two of the publishing phase, we start
> reading the next genre.

By overlapping the genre studies, Madhuvanti also connects children's attention to content and mechanics in reading and writing across multiple genres.
This allows children to go back in their writing mind to an almost finished
genre and link it forward to a genre that is just coming around the corner.
This is a Vygotskian (1978, 1986) process of overlapping zones of proximal
development within and across genres. It is also a Brittonian (1982) process
of "shaping at the point of utterance" in both reading and writing.

Grade 4: "Integrating and Balancing Is Always a Challenge"

For grade 4, the challenges of integrating content and mechanics become
somewhat more differentiated and individualized. At this point, some
children move forward quickly in their writing development, while other
children need continued support and guidance as 4th-grade expectations
expand in terms of reading, writing, and content. Sarah Carp teaches the
English strand in a 4th-grade Spanish/English dual-immersion program. She
co-teaches a class of 20 students, of whom approximately 5 are beginning/
intermediate English speakers, 5 are intermediate/advanced English speakers, 5 are balanced bilinguals, and 5 are native English speakers learning
Spanish. Fifteen of the students are Latina/o and 5 are of Anglo-European
origin.

In thinking about mechanics, Sarah uses the terms *conventions* and
conventions of print, and emphasizes the small units of language that form
Gregory's (2008) inside-out approach.

> We [our grade-level team] think of conventions as including spelling
> and punctuation and syntax and word choice. They pertain to syntax

at the word level as well as the sentence level to include complete sentences and run-on sentences or fragments. If I were to explain conventions to my students, it would be that most readers with grade-level competency could understand it—meaning they wouldn't get stuck on the spelling or the syntax or possible multiple interpretations—and that we hold ourselves as writers to that same standard that we as readers would expect.

For her new language learners, Sarah values attention to the basic elements of language for writing development as a common goal for her whole class.

Sarah also sees written language content as essential for meeting the expanded cognitive and linguistic demands of 4th-grade writing.

I see content as the writer's craft—how a writer engages the reader. For example, right now we're writing book reviews and they have to write a hook to engage the reader. This involves figuring out how to build interest and purpose, how to use precise and vivid and descriptive language, elaborating on ideas, organizing ideas, using transitions, making things flow, and being relevant. Mostly, we do not teach content, but prepare them for content by using conversation, probing questions, mentor texts, and graphic organizers before they write, and then help them get their own ideas and message into the parameters of the assignment. I also think of content as not only writing in their own voice but also helping students to adopt new voices in their writing.

Sarah also views content and mechanics integration in 4th-grade as a nuanced process that happens within and between sentences in students' writing.

One element that falls in the middle of content and mechanics is sentence variety. It involves proper mechanics as well as understanding how to write to convey content effectively. For example, one of my students wrote about a character named Peter and wrote, "Peter is nine years old. Peter is a boy. Peter has a little brother." Today, in class, I helped the student edit this piece and we put those sentences all together into one sentence. For 1st-grade, the three sentences would be a perfectly good sentence structure, but for 4th grade, we're guiding students toward using more variety.

In integrating content and mechanics, Sarah juggles attention to the individual needs of her students, while at the same time moving the entire class toward more sophisticated levels of writing. Given that the majority of her students are new language learners, Sarah strongly believes in emphasizing content to encourage the intangibles in writing well—motivation, interest, engagement, confidence.

Developmentally, for new language learners, Sarah's philosophy connects back to kindergarten, where new language learners (as seen in Florence's kindergarten class) thrive on meaning and content as the foundation for learning grade-level mechanics.

> Integrating and balancing content and mechanics is always a challenge, but the way I've been approaching it, as a 4th-grade teacher, is focusing on content first and just getting the ideas down through graphic organizers. I tell my students not to worry about the spelling, mechanics, or the punctuation. They can use fragments or phrases rather than conventional full sentences, and then create a draft. At this point, I don't over-teach mechanics so that they don't worry too much about correctness because I think it can be stifling sometimes. We then revisit the mechanics through the revision and editing process that can involve peer revisions and peer editing. But it's important first for my students to become invested and excited about their ideas before they are motivated to correct their writing and make it come across clearly and comprehensibly.

Personal investment and motivation are key intangibles in strengthening content and mechanics integration for Sarah's new language learners.

> In editing and revising, I always consider students' feelings and how hurtful it can be sometimes to see that red pen all over the paper. I don't even think they learn from the correcting of every mistake. I think it flattens their motivation. So I try to avoid the red pen and use another color. It's just so jarring. We also try to edit for only one thing at a time. We practice editing with checklists. I'll say, "Reread your whole piece and just look for periods. Reread the whole thing and look for capitals. Reread the whole thing and look for spelling."

At 4th grade, the editing process (which I cover in Chapter 5) has a more prominent position in integrating content and mechanics, and Sarah wants to strengthen her students' positive feelings toward their writing by avoiding early over-editing. The key goal is "not to flatten their motivation," and to give 4th-grade new language learners an early balance between the intangibles and tangibles of content/mechanics integration.

As I wrote this chapter, I read *Duke Ellington: The Piano Prince and His Orchestra* (1999) by Andrea Davis Pinkney (author) and Brian Pinkey Pinkney (illustrator) to Toby, my 5-year-old son. As I read the book to him, I noticed the ways that Andrea Pinkney integrated content and mechanics in the text. The writing mimicked the music of Duke Ellington and the language of his time. Toby listened for and to the story—experiencing the intangible joy of learning about and experiencing the story of a fascinating and talented musician. As I looked more closely at the text to see how Pinkney created such an engaging story, I saw engaging content—the telling of a famous musician's life—and also mechanics that aren't always traditional and conventional.

> And to celebrate the history of African-American people, Duke composed a special suite he called "Black, Brown, and Beige." A suite that rocked the bosom and lifted the soul. (Pinkney, 1999, p. 25)

Pinkney's first sentence starts with "And" and her second sentence could be seen as a sentence fragment. These are examples of mechanics often considered "no-no's," but they work so well here in Pinkney's book. They work because they strengthen the overall voice of the book, its style and tone, and fit the content of its subject—the jazzy, quick, smooth sound of Duke Ellington.

In this chapter, I've presented key ideas and strategies regarding content and mechanics integration from seven talented teachers of writing across the K–4 spectrum. Their perspectives give us a long developmental look at the possibilities for this integration, and also a deep pedagogical picture of powerful ways to conceptualize and implement content/mechanics integration to help children write well.

Chapter 3

PLANNING

I have at last bored down into my oil well, and can't scribble fast enough
to bring it all to the surface. I have now at least 6 stories welling up in
me, and feel, at last, that I can coin all my thoughts into words. Not but
what an infinite number of problems remain; but I have never felt this
rush and urgency before.

—Virginia Woolf, *A Writer's Diary*

For Virginia Woolf, her stories are "welling up" inside her writing mind, and she is at a point where she "can coin all her thoughts into words." Although she is aware of future roadblocks, "the infinite number of problems remaining," Woolf knows that the key movement into writing involves powerful ideas and stories coming through her writing mind, and their transfer into "words" and onto the written page.

Young writers need to find something akin to Woolf's "welling up" of words and ideas, and they also need to find suitable elements of form to give shape to their content. As Ken Macrorie (1984) points out, "readers need some form or they become confused, get lost, give up. Making anything—a table, a fishing fly, a piece of writing—involves a struggle between form and content" (p. 120).

There are, however, a few important caveats to the process of planning to write. First, we can't deceive ourselves as teachers and we can't deceive young writers that excellent planning always leads to good writing. Second, planning *is* actual writing and not a separate step or phase. When we brainstorm on paper, talk with others, draw, use graphic organizers, reread a text or our old writing, or just sit and think, we are actually writing, although we may not always be producing actual written text at a particular moment. Third, not all students always need to plan because the act of writing and composing is such a creative and cognitively rich process that new feelings and ideas often arise later on when young writers compose.

We need, then, to remain flexible and not hold all young writers to the same planning routines and expectations. As the writer Vendela Vida explains, "I'm not the kind of writer who sketches everything out. I like to be surprised by where the character takes me" (Guthrie, 2009). And the author Wells Tower (Low, 2010) also notes, "Story kernels take different forms. . . . Sometimes, I'll think I've got a short story all but written in my head, and when I sit down at the keyboard, it disintegrates. Other times, I'll think I'm sketching an image or joke, or a notion for a character, and it metastasizes into a story. It rarely happens the same way twice."

So much of effective planning involves taking the time to think, absorbing one's ideas and thoughts, letting feelings come to us, collecting our resources, and giving time to plan before actual composing. And even then, the planning process can vary each time.

THEORETICAL REMINDERS

Several researchers from Chapter 1 provide important theoretical reminders for conceptualizing and supporting children's planning for writing.

Knowledge of Language Forms

Lisa Delpit (1986, 1988, 1992, 2002) reminds us that some children of color and other children who have experienced a lack of access to mainstream forms of written language benefit from direct and sensitive guidance in forms of written language. This means that we can't always assume that young writers will know the forms and genres that we are asking them to plan for, and they need our direct support to recognize, mimic, and internalize these forms and structures. This knowledge constitutes an essential part of what Delpit calls "expert knowledge" that children need to recognize, control, and internalize essential forms and functions of powerful writing. For some children, knowledge of these forms starts early in their home and community learning. For those children who may not be exposed to this background knowledge, school-based instruction must focus on providing this invaluable background knowledge of key elements of written language structures and genres.

Development and Symbol Systems

Anne Haas Dyson (1986, 1989, 1993, 2003) shows us that learning to write is a dynamic process that takes in all of children's knowledge of symbol systems and ways to embed writing in the social and intellectual fabric of classroom life. In this dynamic view of children's writing development, children dip back and move forward as they gain greater orchestration over understanding and manipulating symbol systems of drawing and writing. So planning for writing is a key part of this developmental back and forth, and rich opportunities for young writers also include talking and interacting with peers and adults. If we see content and mechanics integration as a central way for children to represent themselves and their worlds in writing, then children need to get ideas and responses from others as they plan. In this view, it is not only the final written product that does something for young writers—it is also the early process of planning, talking, interacting, and thinking.

New Language Learners

For María de la luz Reyes (1992) and Katharine Samway (2006), new language learners benefit from support in their primary languages, and this can often help young writers get started. This is evident in bilingual classrooms, dual-immersion classes, and in English language development classes. For instance, Florence Tse uses Chinese to support her mostly Chinese-speaking kindergarten students as they plan and think about their writing. Sarah Carp, teaching the English half of a Spanish/English immersion 4th grade, uses her Spanish as needed to support her students to brainstorm and think about their writing. New language learners also benefit from direct support in vocabulary and syntax at the planning stage, so they have a lexus of words and possible syntactical structures before they compose. This provides essential linguistic background knowledge and decreases the chance of linguistic and cognitive overload during composing.

Eve Gregory (2001) shows how new language learners learn specific "cultural knowledge" through "cultural routines" in the home and community. In terms of planning for writing, it is helpful when new language learners have access to familiar cultural knowledge and routines. One critical way to achieve this support for planning is through an integration of Gregory's (2008) inside-out (comprised of small units of language) and outside-in (comprised of larger units such as stories) approaches. Young writers, then, plan effectively for writing when they think about how to put together small and large units of language before they are too deep into the composing process.

POTENTIAL STUMBLING BLOCKS

To deeply understand the process of planning for writing, it's helpful to consider the challenges in terms of content and mechanics for young writers.

Content

In terms of content, young writers may:

- feel that they have nothing to say
- not know where to start with a first word or sentence
- not understand the content of the writing assignment or activity
- feel they've written it before
- want to be so creative and original that any start is not good enough
- know where they want to go but not know where to start
- start off with an idea but then forget it as they start composing
- start with a good idea but then lose interest
- feel that their picture or drawing already says everything they want to say, and there's nothing more to say in a written text

Mechanics

In terms of mechanics, young writers may:

- believe or know that they don't know how to spell enough words to write what they want to
- believe that they can write only using the words they can spell (i.e., their spelling skills dictate the direction and content of their writing)
- believe that invented spelling is too much linguistic and cognitive work, and so they stick only to words they know how to spell
- feel that it's simply too tiring physically to write a lot or for a long period of time
- have an idea of what they want to write but lack the vocabulary and skill to make changes to words to fit the syntax of a given phrase or sentence
- feel or know that it's a struggle to make spaces between the words and/or follow a left-to-right and return sweep
- not understand the format, genre, or structure of a specific writing assignment or activity
- have a global sense of the format or genre but are unable to break it down into its constituent parts to know where to start
- have an insufficient grasp of an author's style if the writing is designed to mimic or integrate elements of a certain author
- not know how long it will take to write a particular piece or part

- feel attached to a particular personal style and be unwilling to forego it in favor of following a particular teacher's emphasis on mechanics

Individual Preferences

These stumbling blocks can be present in different configurations for individual children across the K–4 span. They also differ because individual young writers have their own preferences and styles. For example, I asked Kaili, a 4th-grader, about her personal style for sentence writing.

> I like writing long sentences because I like the way they look and I like the way they sound. I don't like choppy sentences that are short like "She wanted a watermelon. So she went to the store. Then, she bought one," as oppposed to, "She wanted a watermelon, so she went to the store and bought one." This second sentence just sounds much smoother and the words flow into each other. If kids are having trouble writing like this, just replace a period with a comma to make longer sentences, but be sure not to make them run-on sentences, as this is the only flaw with longer sentences.

Effective Strategies

The theoretical ideas presented in Chapter 1 help us conceptualize a theoretical framework for content and mechanics integration. Chapter 2 shows us how we can define content and mechanics and fit their integration into our teaching philosophies and writing curriculum. There are several additional strategies to help young writers get started in their writing:

- Allow extended periods of time for planning, brainstorming, and thinking.
- Allow opportunities for young writers to converse and check in with peers to get ideas.
- Make ourselves available for talking with young writers to help them start.
- Use visuals, graphic organizers, charts, and other resources to trigger ideas and provide background knowledge.
- Allow flexible use of graphic organizers; some young writers don't like to be hemmed in by too much initial planning that they feel they must follow.
- Use manipulatives (like Post-its) so young writers can jot down ideas and move them around until they find a pleasing sequence or structure for their piece as they plan and compose.

- Provide frequent mini-lessons or other forms of structured guidance on how to get started.
- Confer or check in early and often with those young writers most in need of support in getting started.
- Continually point out useful vocabulary and syntactical structures in read-alouds, guided reading texts, independent reading texts, and children's own writing.
- Help children review and revisit prior writing to see whether they want to continue what they've been working on or write something new.

When used in combination, and fine-tuned over time, these ideas and strategies help young writers get started with their writing, and help them see and feel that planning *is* writing and an inseparable part of writing well.

PLANNING AS WRITING

There are several powerful ways that young writers can integrate content and mechanics in their planning. These include linking drawing, talking, and writing; structured lessons; and linking reading and writing.

Drawing, Talking, and Writing: Resources for Planning

Young writers, especially those at the K–1 level but also at times in grades 2–4, benefit from a foundation of experiences talking, interacting, and drawing. Vygotsky's (1978, 1986) ideas on the Zone of Proximal Development (ZPD) show us how the integration of content and mechanics relates to the dance between what young writers plan on drawing and writing and what they actually compose. Access to talking, interaction, and drawing—a key Vygotskian idea—helps young writers in the sociocultural and cognitive challenge of integrating content and mechanics. When we help young writers plan well, then we stretch out and deepen their ZPDs for this integration—helping them see an ample range of writing possibilities (the spreading out dynamic) and ways to write with depth of thought, feeling, and description (the deepening dynamic).

This developmentally valuable trio—talking, interacting, and drawing—is intimately linked to key intersections between children's language and intellectual development. James Britton (1987) notes that Vygotsky's four central ideas underlie this intimate linkage:

1. "Word meanings *evolve* during childhood" [original emphasis] and vocabulary develops through daily communication.

2. Children learn through spontaneous (i.e., what is learned through human deduction) and non-spontaneous concepts (i.e., what is learned through constructivist learning).
3. The "*constancy* of written language is grafted . . . upon the *immediacy* of spoken language" [original emphasis], which promotes reflection on language and thought.
4. Conversation helps children "extend their control of the grammatical structures of the spoken language and increase their resources of conventional word-meaning" (p. 23)—that is, syntactical and vocabulary knowledge increases through talking with peers and adults.

Vygotsky also helps us see how planning for writing can be supported through drawing and making marks and symbols. According to Britton (1983), Vygotsky linked speech and context, and saw context as the "here-and-now" of "cooperative behavior" with others (p. 14). As children experience "represented experiences" using and interpreting symbols in books and drawings, the context for children's learning "expands" and "the child reaches a stage where the remembered experience" can be brought to bear on a task or activity (p. 14). A developmental leap happens when a child "draws what he *knows* rather than what he can see and he musters that knowledge in speaking as he draws" (p. 15). This process becomes even more sophisticated when children use speech to describe and explain their drawing, and children sense that they can draw their thinking *and* their language.

Drawing becomes an important form of planning for young writers as they link their ideas, feelings, and images with corresponding words, names, phrases, and sentences. It also becomes a developmental bridge between two-dimensional (drawing) and three-dimensional (real-life) space—as Toby, a 5-year-old, said, "Sometimes it's easier to show something than say it. And if you draw something really well, it sometimes might come to life."

Drawing and other marks are also a window onto children's strategies and problem-solving for understanding and using symbols to represent experience, objects, and ideas. For example, Marie Clay's (1975) basic principles for their early writing (Recurring, Directional, Generating, Inventory, Contrastive, Abbreviation) as discussed in Chapter 1 help us see early developmental linkages between drawing, symbolic representation, and writing.

Drawing is also a developmental precursor for the motoric aspects of planning for writing. As Janet Emig (1983) observed, "we see and hear, as we move our hands, with our brain" (p. 111). The hand influences planning through

1. "the literal act of writing" as "activating" (p. 111)
2. making composing an aesthetic process
3. possibly influencing the "linear aspects of the brain" (p. 112)
4. writing by hand, which "keeps the process slowed down" (p. 112)

According to Emig, the human eye is necessary for planning, composing, and revision:

1. prewriting ("presenting experience to the brain")
2. writing ("the eye coordinates the hand and brain for most of us")
3. revision ("the eye is the major instrument by which we rescan and review what we have written") (p. 113)

When we integrate drawing and other forms of visual representation into the planning process, these elements support the physical elements of writing well across the writing process.

Kindergarten: Representing Meaning While Learning Mechanics

"Guess what I'm drawing?" 5-year-old Mia asked me as she started to draw. Her question highlights the intentionality and direction that drawing can elicit. And before young writers can write conventionally, or even form letters as a form of scribble scrabble, they can use drawing to experience and practice planning out what they might want to represent in form and meaning. By asking her question, Mia gains valuable practice in thinking out loud and engaging an adult in *predicting* drawing content. In a Vygotskian sense, as outlined in Chapter 1, Mia's question is a form of external speech for others that strengthens her internal speech and her internal ideas and thoughts for the content and shape of her drawing.

In another example, I sat beside 5-year-old Talia as she drew and said, "This is the ground. This is a big tree. There, there's a sloth hanging from a tree." Talia talks to herself, to her drawing, and to me. In this way, she uses speech as a *parallel linguistic process*, which provides valuable early practice for her later development when she will plan out loud what she plans to write.

In another example, 5-year-olds Abigail and Relnisha were drawing similar pictures side by side as they talked about their drawing.

Abigail: I'm making grass.
Relnisha: I'm making me a backyard.
Abigail: That's his hair. (draws on Relnisha's page) That's your cat and that's your dog. (again draws on Relnisha's page) I have to make my puppy.

Relnisha: I made me a seesaw.
Abigail: That's a big big whale.
Relnisha: I'm going to make me a moon.
Abigail: That's the whale.
Relnisha: Wait a second, we're not done yet. Look at my sun. You
like my sun?

As Abigail and Relnisha comment and draw on one another's papers, they engage in a "planning-as-we-go" collaboration and learn to recognize one another's particular content and mechanics. For Abigail and Relnisha, and other children who are not yet writing conventionally, drawing allows them to "say" things that they can't say yet in writing.

Rickey, another kindergartner with whom I worked, used his drawings to connect with texts. In his journals for writing and drawing, he liked to copy sentences and draw pictures from books after flipping through them for interesting pictures. For example, in early December, he wrote "sometime squirrels" from the beginning of a sentence in a book about squirrels and drew a picture of a flying squirrel (Figure 3.1). Rickey links his written text with the drawing, and both are integrated as they are in the model of the text and picture in the squirrel book.

Figure 3.1. Rickey's Squirrel Drawing and Writing

Visual images are a powerful trigger for writing, and can help young writers identify a beginning structure and content for writing. As the children's author Allen Say notes:

> Usually, my books start with a very vague notion or idea. Then I begin to draw things that come into my mind. Eventually, I see a pattern within the pictures. It is this pattern that develops into a tentative plot. My next step is to complete all my paintings for the book. After they are finished, I write the story. This may seem like the reverse of what appears to be the natural storytelling process, but for me, the plot of the story develops through the pictures. . . . I often go for walks to look for ideas. Ideas are what I call "found objects." I can see them with the naked eye or visualize them in my mind. Finding ideas is a process of feeding one's mind with seemingly unrelated images and information. Then these things spark a thought or a progression of thoughts. (Loer, n.d.)

Young writers like Rickey are at the cusp of Allen Say's planning and creative process—creating visuals and pictures to prompt an unfolding story or piece of writing. The pictures that Rickey finds in a book are akin to Allen Say's "found objects."

Since picture books have a *built-in* integration of text and picture, they provide Rickey with a model of integrating content and mechanics as he is learning to write conventionally. As Lucy Calkins (1986) notes, "The act of drawing and the picture itself both provide a supportive scaffolding within which the piece of writing can be constructed" (p. 50).

By late spring, Rickey continued to be motivated to integrate drawing and writing, and his spelling, handwriting, syntax, and confidence were all stronger. In late May, he drew a dragon from a book on dragons and I helped him write a sentence: "I like dragon becs they blow fiwr" (Figure 3.2). Rickey was a careful artist, first drawing the outline of the dragon in pencil and then using the green and red markers to bring his fire-breathing dragon to life. The picture gave Rickey solid content to write from, and the book's text gave him correct word spellings (he copied the word *dragon*) and also language to connect to the pictures.

Since I worked with a small group of kindergartners, I could work closely with Rickey on mechanics. I also wanted to give Rickey direct instruction on *mechanics orchestration*, which involved these elements:

- forming the letters, and choosing between lower- and uppercase letters
- organizing his writing spatially on the page
- paying attention to the syntactical structures of his phrases and sentences
- remembering what he wanted to write

Figure 3.2. Rickey's Dragon Drawing and Writing

- helping him make any changes mid-sentence in his ideas and then adjusting for spelling any new words and forming the letters
- writing with a healthy mix of transitional spelling *and* conventional spelling
- paying attention to punctuation in the book and in his writing

As I helped him write "I like dragon becs they blow fiwr," I estimated which elements of mechanics he did not need any help with, which he needed some support with, and those that demanded most of my support. In terms of spelling, I knew Rickey could spell the word *I* on his own and knew the beginning sound/letter of *like, dragon, because, blow,* and *fire,* but would need help with all of the word *they* and also the medial and ending sounds in most of the words in the sentence. I gave Rickey small hints and cues to help him spell as I did the following:

- extended the word a few times and accented the vowel or consonant sound he needed to write the corresponding letter(s) (he wrote "b-l-o" and I then told him it ended with "w")

- provided the correct sound and then waited to see if Rickey knew the corresponding letter (as in the letter for "n" in *dragon*)
- told Rickey the letter name but let him figure out how to write the letter (as in the "g" for *dragon*)
- told Rickey, "It's either a __ or it's a __" (either "k" or "c" for *like*)
- directly told him the correct letter or letter combination (the "ey" in *they*)
- pointed out something problematic ("the /zee/ sound at the end of *because* sounds like a 'z' but it's actually spelled with an 's'")
- decided not to press for the full, accurate spelling of a word (I decided to let *because* go as "becs" because Rickey had written enough letters for someone to read it back recognizably as *because*)
- he added a "w" for "fiwr" (*fire*), which I let go since it was his last word, and the word *fire* almost sounds like it could have a "w" in it

I used these strategies to help Rickey orchestrate his *intra*-sentence mechanics. If he had written more than one sentence, possibly to tell a story about a dragon or give more information on dragons, then I would have needed to support Rickey's *inter*-sentence mechanics orchestration as well, and gone back and forth between the two levels of syntactical structures and Rickey's evolving content. As it was, writing one sentence demanded a lot of Rickey's energy and concentration, and he was proud of his accomplishment.

Structured Lessons: Conscious Preparation to Write

While some kindergarten and 1st-grade children are ready to consciously plan their writing, in general older children are more able to do so. Graves (1994) notes the value of preparing for writing.

> Conscious rehearsal accompanies the decision to write. Rehearsal refers to the preparation for composing and can take the form of daydreaming, sketching, doodling, making lists of words, outlining, reading, conversing, or even writing lines as a foil to further rehearsal. (p. 76)

A critical part of this conscious preparation is children's choice of writing topics and frequent opportunities for planning and choosing their writing content.

> When students write every day they don't find it as difficult to choose topics. If a child knows she will write again tomorrow, her mind can go to work pondering her writing topic. Choosing a topic once a week is difficult. The moment for writing suddenly arrives, and the mind is caught unprepared. (Graves, 1994, p. 106)

Children are also successful in choosing topics and in planning their writing when they have a greater sense of responsibility for their planning. Young writers will have "their ups and downs as writers, but these will occur within the context of personal involvement in writing" (Calkins, 1986, p. 6). Not only is topic choice central to this personal investment, but young writers also benefit from choosing "their own form, voice, and audience" and taking "ownership and responsibility for their writing" (p. 6).

As Delpit (1986, 1988, 1998, 2002), Reyes (1992), Samway (2006), and others remind us, though, young writers also need direct support and guidance in understanding, recognizing, and appropriating written language conventions. Delpit (1998) argues that we "need to support the language that students bring to school, provide them with input from an additional code, and give them the opportunity to use the new code in a nonthreatening, real communicative context" (p. 53).

Effective planning, then, must include sensitive and thoughtful ways for children to know the key elements in a certain written language form or genre before composing. This "acquiring of an additional code" occurs when children connect "the language form with all that is self-affirming and esteem-building, inviting and fun" (Delpit, 2002, p. 39). Effective planning for writing also involves children's "most intimate expressions of identity, indeed, 'the skin that we speak'" (p. 47) as our direct guidance goes beyond mere mechanics and form to touch children's identities and views of themselves as writers and learners.

New language learners also need particular support in recognizing written language structures and formats, finding the right vocabulary and content for planning their writing, and organizing their thoughts and feelings in a new language (Gregory, 2008). Successful planning for writing, then, provides new language learners with "just enough" content and mechanics knowledge and integration to begin the composing process and have a tentative road map for where they are going.

Mini-Lessons and Structured Guidance

Mini-lessons, involving 5–10 minutes of guided instruction to a small group or whole class, are a particularly valuable place for focusing on mechanics and showing young writers how they can be integrated with content.

> The purpose of the mini-lesson is to help children understand the meaning of conventions and begin a list of the ones they are already using. I usually conduct a mini-lesson with an entire class; then I'll move to work with a small group of children who I suspect have difficulty understanding the conventions. (Graves, 1994, p. 193)

Mini-lessons are also valuable for new language learners, especially those without frequent access to speakers of their primary language.

> In classes where the teacher may be the only (or almost only) target-language speaker, s/he will need to be constantly alive to his/her role as language model, carefully considering vital "chunks" of language needed, initiating and practising them in a variety of spoken and written contexts. (Gregory, 2008, p. 168)

Mini-lessons support the planning of new language learners by breaking down written language into bite-size chunks, and showing young writers a reasonable place to start and continue working on their writing.

For her 1st-graders, Ilsa Miller uses mini-lessons or, as she calls them, "structured lessons," to help her students plan elements of content and mechanics in their writing. Ilsa uses a combination of Eve Gregory's (2008) inside-out and outside-in approaches as she focuses on chunks of language and larger text forms or structures such as stories. Ilsa decides on the focus of these lessons depending on what she sees her students needing at a particular moment.

> I plan the structured lessons ahead of time and then teach them on a day-by-day basis as I'm reading student writing and seeing if there's something that it seems several children need to work on. The children's work in progress focuses my lessons. For example, it might be that they're all beginning their stories with "once upon a time." I may change my weekly plans and add an unplanned lesson on story openings. In a good month, I plan big chunks, and then I plan by the week and I change it day-by-day if my plans don't seem applicable to what the students are writing. So I make broad ideas and add if I notice that a lot of the children need something. During independent writing time, I scoot around between all the students using a checklist to make sure that I'm meeting with everyone.

Moving "always with direction and purpose," Ilsa's structured lessons follow a developmental progression from "ideas for writing" to "important mechanics" to "word choice." Ilsa's deliberateness and inclination to adapt lessons as needed keeps her content and mechanics integration in step with moment-by-moment changes in her students' writing. Ilsa, then, follows Nancie Atwell's (1987) apt observation, "I think we teach too many skills and not at the right time" (p. 144).

> Recently, I'm spending a lot of time teaching ideas for stories so that the children know what to write about. For those children who seem

> hesitant to write, I give them a lot of time to think about things they're
> interested in. So I focus on the what and the how. For instance, when
> students are writing choice stories, I may focus on how to end a story.
> I spend time teaching how to plan out a story's beginning, middle, and
> end so that students can see where their story is going and how it will
> end. Some stories seem to go on forever because the writer is under-
> standably unsure about how to end it. So I see mechanics as part of the
> planning of the story. And yet it's also the content. We do a lot of chart-
> ing before starting the story with simple beginning, middle, and end
> maps. I had one student who would often get teary at the beginning of
> the year at writing time. The charts really helped him plan his stories so
> that he knew what he was going to write.

Knowing that her age group of students needs support for writing, especially in starting off with ideas, Ilsa devotes a good deal of time to helping
her "hesitant" students. She knows that the intangible factor of confidence
will improve with attention to the tangible evidence of planning what to
write about.

As an experienced teacher, Ilsa has reached the point where she knows
how to be "deliberate" with her structured lessons for planning, and can
differentiate the needs of individual students and small groups of students.

> For instance with word choice, I can point out the different ways that
> certain students approach choosing words for their writing. I have some
> students in 1st grade who will go to a thesaurus and find a word that is
> just right, and they'll know how to use it in their writing. Other students
> will work on improving sentences like "It was fun" or "I like it" by think-
> ing of a different way to say it.

Ilsa also devotes time in her structured lessons to teaching effective planning
through modeling her own writing. Ilsa's writing-as-modeling especially
helps new language learners and others who benefit from direct attention to
small language chunks as well as large text structures (Gregory, 2008). By
demonstrating close attention to the language she uses in her own writing,
Ilsa avoids two factors that hinder the literacy learning of new language
learners: 1) "they lack personal 'key' or meaningful words in the target
language" and 2) "they are forced to remember every individual word until
they have enough 'chunks' of language at their fingertips" (Gregory, 2008,
p. 160).

Ilsa believes she needs to be interested in her own writing before she
can expect her modeled writing to interest her students. She also knows that

in modeling writing to help students plan their own writing, it is helpful to show how small pieces of experience can turn into something larger.

> When teaching about thinking of ideas for a new story, I often start with mini-lessons about small moments in my life. One time I wrote about when my son got his hand stuck in between a shopping cart and a concrete wall at Costco. I emphasized zooming in on that small moment and made that moment into a story. I emphasized to the class that the key moment is not about what we're getting at Costco, it's not about being at the hospital, it's about that one moment—right before he got hurt, when he got hurt, and right after. I planned out my story for the class in my head and brainstormed all of these ideas aloud with the class.

Ilsa uses a small moment of meaningful human experience and breaks down both the experience and the process of translating this experience into writing. Ilsa also jots down possible writing topics in a small "idea notebook" that her students also have. For example, one page of her notebook has six different possible topics, which she showed to her students. As a model, Ilsa's list contains a developmentally manageable number of topics, and she uses a minimum number of key vocabulary to give the gist of each possible topic.

- Rosie under the car
- Snowstorm—rear-ended
- Dinner with Tony
- Snorkeling
- Getting off the chair lift
- Evan's hand and shopping

Ilsa circled the last topic, deciding she was most interested in writing about and modeling the story of her son's hand injury at Costco. She then wrote down a possible beginning, middle, and end for her story and sketched a brief picture (Figure 3.3).

> I then write ideas down and also draw pictures to help certain students who benefit from visuals. I show them how I am simply writing my ideas down. I'm not writing sentences. I'm not worrying about spelling. I'm just getting my ideas down. I model through thinking out loud how interested I was in writing about Evan's hand because I thought that I would have a lot to write about. It was important to me and I thought it

Figure 3.3. Ilsa's Story Planning Visual

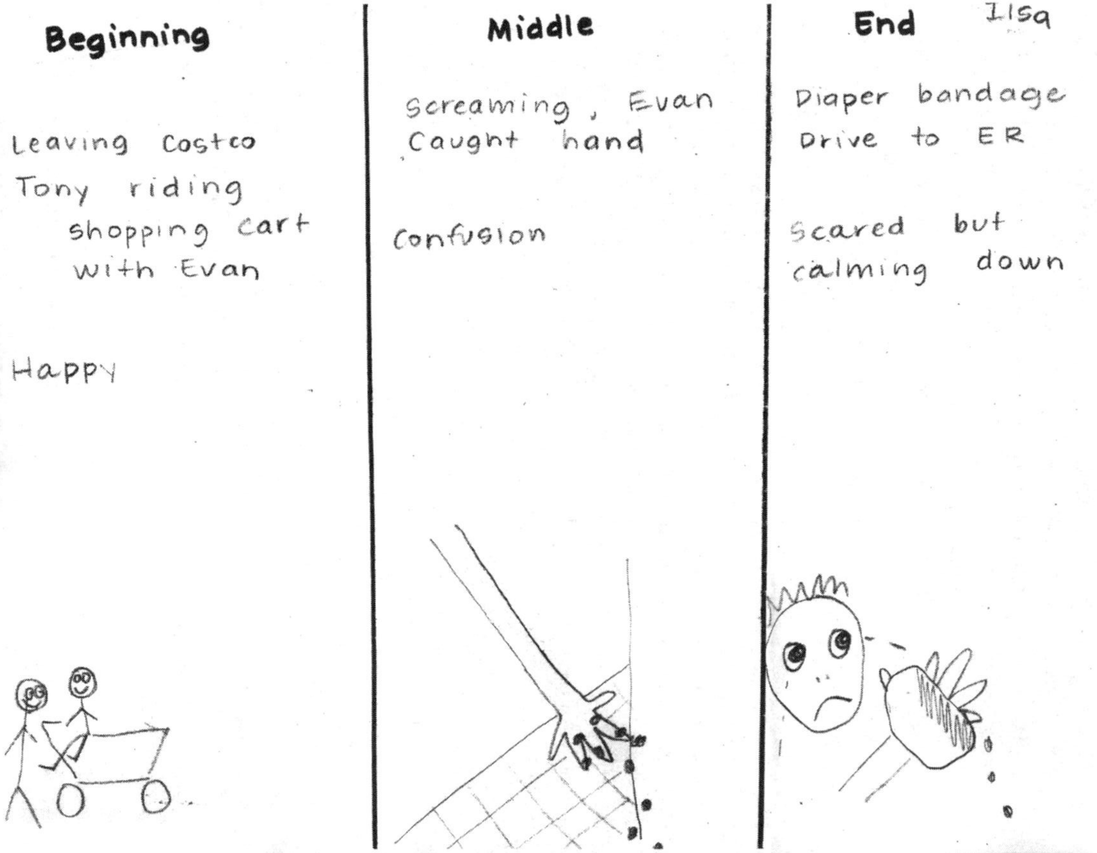

Beginning	Middle	End
Leaving Costco Tony riding shopping cart with Evan	Screaming, Evan Caught hand	Diaper bandage Drive to ER
Happy	Confusion	Scared but calming down
		Ilsa

was something that would interest the class. I also talk with them about audience, too. I share that I think about whom I'm writing for, and by watching their expressions as I was telling them about Evan's hand, it made me think that they'd like to hear and see me write about that moment.

Ilsa's planning sheet provides ideas for the content of her impending story as well as mechanics that include a beginning-middle-end story structure, key vocabulary words, and spelling. Her sheet also efficiently models for her students key elements of powerful narrative writing. John Dixon and Leslie Stratta (1986) note four essential elements of narrative writing: particularities of human experience, time and an unfolding plot, context of setting and characters, and an overall integration of experience, time, and context. Ilsa's sheet lays out Dixon and Stratta's elements of experience, time, and context, and then, in the next step of composing, Ilsa can integrate these three elements.

As Ilsa writes her story with her students watching and listening, she refers back to her planning sheet for reference. As she does so, Ilsa's students become her audience and she looks at their reactions and gauges what to say and write as she goes. Her written piece (Figure 3.4) uses text and two sketches to flesh out the beginning, middle, and end elements from her planning sheet. To model syntactical variation, Ilsa varies the length and style of her sentences, and uses conventional spelling and punctuation. She will occasionally toss in a spelling, punctuation, or stylistic error as she writes, and she enlists the children's help in finding errors when they reread and edit the piece together: "hs" corrected as "His," "wAs" corrected as "was," "i" changed to "me," "withadiaper" changed to "with a diaper," and "emrgncy" changed to "emergency." Ilsa also helps her students see other possibilities for word choice in their rereading (as she changed "pinched" to the more specific and hurtful "jammed" and also "really scraped" to the more serious "severely scraped").

Ilsa believes that this kind of integration of planning and composing with her students is "the most engaging way to go," and she makes on-the-spot changes to strengthen the connections.

> If students begin to lose interest, I'll stop or model aloud the need for making a change in my story, but it really gets quiet and the class just wants to know what happened next. The next day, they're really interested in the mini-lesson because they want to know the next part of the story and what will happen. I don't write too much so that they have their own ideas. The next step is to model and solicit ideas from my students about how to turn the planning chart ideas into sentences and a

Figure 3.4. Ilsa's Story

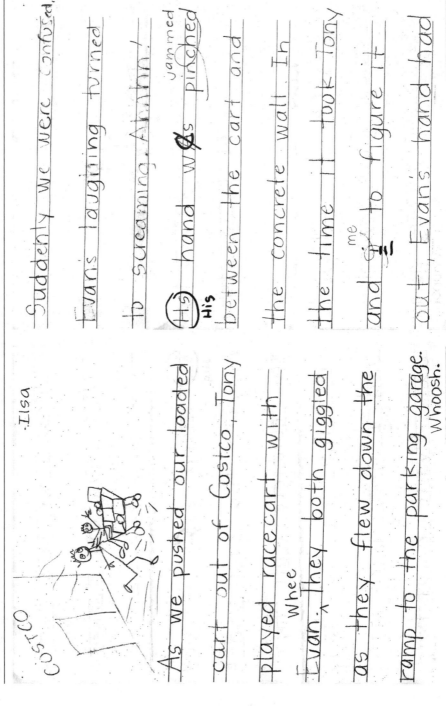

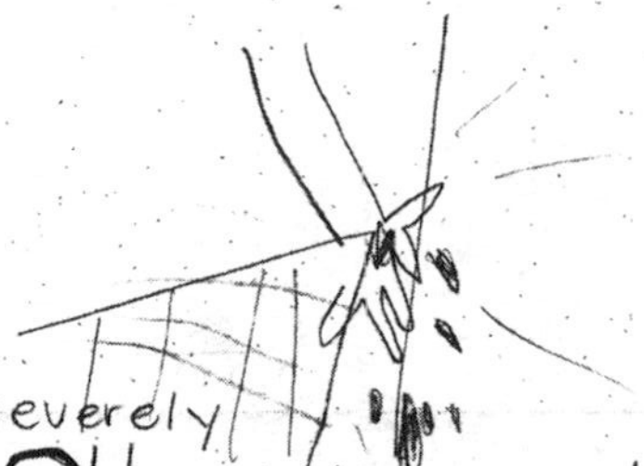

car, leaving our groceries,

and rushed to the

emrgncy room.
emergency

been really ~~scraped~~. severely
~~really~~

Blood was everywhere.

Tony thought quickly

and bandaged Evan's

hand with a diaper. We

whisked Evan to the

full story. The next day, they set to writing after we review how the planning chart was used to make sentences and add more details, stressing
again that the chart is not your finished story, but just three parts of it.
For example, Jake set to work and ended up writing, "When I was on
vacation I was throwing rocks and one landed on my head. The doctors
came. I went to the hospital and got staples in my head. Ow. Then two
days later I got my staples out. It hurts. Now it's like normal." This story
was a big deal for Jake because he came from a place of being teary
when it was writing time and having difficulty finishing a story.

Jake's planning sheet (Figure 3.5) shows just enough content and mechanics
to get him going on his story.

- Beginning: rain weekly, throw rocks
- Middle: rock land on head, big cut, long drive
- End: staples

Figure 3.5. Jake's Planning Sheet

For his drawings, he draws rain and rocks falling on people (beginning), a figure crying (middle), and a figure on a stretcher (end).

In his written piece (Figure 3.6), Jake makes use of both the content and mechanics of his planning sheet. His planning sheet provided just enough story ideas with a chronology (content) and key words, phrases, and spellings (mechanics) for Jake to flesh out a well-rounded, engaging story in only 48 total words. (I return to the editing of Jake's piece in Chapter 5.)

How has Ilsa's planning helped Jake and her other students? By starting with an experience of personal interest, breaking down elements of her experience, jotting down ideas and key vocabulary, drawing pictures, writing down phrases and words instead of full sentences, writing down ideas in a particular order, writing only part of her potential story, and carrying her writing across more than 1 day, Ilsa provides a real-life model of planning for writing. Along the way, Ilsa's modeling shows how content (ideas, feelings, experiences, problems, solutions, action, events) can be integrated with mechanics (story structure, key vocabulary, key phrases, sequencing, spelling, syntactical structures, punctuation).

Given the need for varied "entry points" into writing (Glover, 2009), we need to provide our own varied models of our own writing as planning. This means that we need to anticipate and plan for certain elements of content and mechanics that reach each of our students. We need, then, to continually adapt what we write (content), how we write it (mechanics), and what we say about it (conscious level of content and mechanics integration) to provide an entry point for each child.

READING AND WRITING: KEY CONNECTIONS FOR PLANNING

Kindergarten

For her class of mostly new language learners, Florence Tse uses high-quality read-alouds to help her students plan their writing. In relying especially on books with patterned text and a well-told story, Florence uses Eve Gregory's (2008) outside-in approach, which involves using stories to help children identify and incorporate larger chunks of language into their writing.

For the first 3 months of kindergarten, Florence helps her students create interactive writing books that she uses in her reader's workshop. As mentioned in Chapter 2, these books start with interactive drawings (pictures the children draw of each other). To then add text, Florence uses interactive writing (Mermelstein, 2006), where Florence writes down each child's oral text and the children write what letters they can. The books then become part of the children's reader's workshop as texts to memorize

Figure 3.6. Jake's Rock Story

Jake   e la sar as hon head   edited
                                                      by
                                                      Ursula

"Wen I was on vocadon
I was throuing rocks

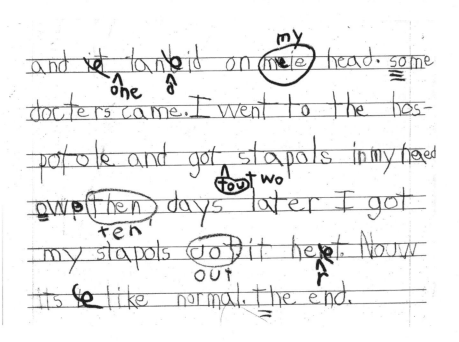

                                          my
and it lanbid on mie head. some
        one a
docters came. I went to the hos-
potole. and got stapols in my head
                    fout wo
awe then days later I got
        ten
my stapols do it here. Nouw
              out
its le like normal. the end.

and read. The interactive books inspire a "sense of ownership" and some "children actually recommend the books to each other." The interactive books "blur the lines" between reading and writing and let "the similarities *enhance* or improve . . . and the difference *complement* [original emphasis] or add to" both reading and writing (Mermelstein, 2006, p. 25).

Third Grade

Joli Gordon helps her students plan for writing by linking it to their reading. Exemplifying Gregory's (2008) outside-in approach, Joli begins the school year by motivating her students to write in their writer's notebook.

> For about the first month of school, my students are not composing anything formally. They're not ready for a project yet. I introduce the idea of the writer's notebook and I get them really jazzed about writing so I share excerpts from my own writer's notebook the first week of school, which consists of diary entries, lists, ideas, doodles, poetry, and quotes. By the second week, I read from the *Amelia's Notebook* series (Moss, 2006) and other notebook-type writing and invite former students to share their old notebooks. In their notebooks, they are not expected to write a whole story; they can really write anything they want, and it can even be a drawing. Then we have Writer's Notebook Day, which is a huge celebration where we all have our notebooks ready to share and then we get to write. We imagine how our favorite authors might have gotten their ideas to write and find out how their lives gave them plenty of ideas to write about. And then eventually I say, "You know, you might have a little drawing there or it could be a word or the beginning of a story and that is going to become your seed idea" and I make a big deal about your seed idea for a bigger project. I also tell them, "When you commit to a seed idea, it must be something that you're very passionate about." So we spend a lot of time processing the planning process. I want it cemented in.

Joli also anchors the larger reading-writing connection within structured activities and guidance regarding specific reading strategies and genres.

> When students come to me in 3rd grade, many have a "one size fits all" approach to reading that one reads informational text the same way one would read a story, and that you're either a "good" reader or a "bad" reader. I then model, emphasize, and review strategic reading— that strategic readers read differently depending on the genre, on one's own background knowledge, and the purpose of a particular text. I

organize my reading curriculum by genres, highlighting particular authors in the first semester and social studies topics in the second semester. I make the genres really specific and we practice a lot of the different reading strategies that we eventually transfer over to our writing.

Joli's curricular integration nicely echoes Leah Mermelstein's (2006) emphasis on the power of linking reading and writing to promote a range of effective literacy strategies—learning to make decisions independently, activating relevant prior knowledge, ascertaining key content in texts, making inferences from texts, imagining and visualizing text content, synthesizing content, asking questions and reflecting, self-monitoring, and activating knowledge of language chunks and mechanics.

In the second half of her year, Joli deepens the reading-writing connection by building on her students' outside-in (Gregory, 2008) narrative experiences from earlier in the year.

In the second semester, the reading is connected more with "content"— not that the first semester isn't. It differs because first semester, it's more about getting into the story, a format that students from the lower grades are more familiar with, and not that there isn't any content in stories, but for content I am referring to reading for information (science, social studies, math, etc.). These areas serve a different purpose than reading for pleasure, which I emphasized more in the first semester. For stories, it involves getting into the plot, connecting with the characters, losing yourself in the book, and learning and experiencing how good readers read and the types of behaviors good readers exhibit. For example, I ask, "What do we do when we come to a word and we're stuck on that word?" That's what we practice first semester, and then second semester we build on the reading from the first semester—we do lots of reader's theater, drama, and visualizing that translates into their writing. If I have students that are stuck on describing a certain part of their story, I'll have them act it out. In the first semester, my students work on a story project, and in the second semester, they complete a research project.

Joli's linking of reading and writing through "crossover" reading/writing strategies and genres pays off later in the year as her students plan and write texts that are information-based and connected to curriculum content. By doing this, Joli avoids the pitfall of "planning our reading and writing curriculum calendars separately" and "hiding the connection from our students" (Mermelstein, 2006, p. 91).

PLANNING FOR WRITING: IT CAN START AS A SPECK

"Different Water"
Water isn't always
A trickle from the eye.
Sometimes it's a crystal
Clear tsunami killing
One thousand at a time.
It can start as a speck,
A dot, but it's huge all
The same. It is very
Powerful, as powerful
As the words on this page.

—Nate Koch (Age 8,
Denver, Colorado.
Teacher: Linda Keller.)

Nate's poem encapsulates the theme of this chapter—that powerful planning for writing involves an integration of content and mechanics. Young writers need engaging ideas, experiences, thoughts, insights, puzzles, and problems to get going in their planning and start their writing. They need, as the narrator in Nate's poem did, an experience such as the tsunami that left so much destruction and death that words can barely approach its ramifications for us. At the same time, young writers need access to "words on a page" to render at least part of that experience, at least part of that idea or feeling—the "speck" that turns "very powerful" both on and off the page.

The theorists, teachers, and young writers featured in this chapter show us how and why planning *is* writing, and help us link a "speck" or "dot" of experience with arrays of possible "words on a page." This is essentially what planning for or getting ready to write involves—a potential plan or idea or feeling that gathers some semblance of shape and order. It gathers just enough steam to move forward into potentially new movements, new adventures, new shapes. Planning gives us the first few steps. And from there we carry on, adjusting and tinkering with ways to integrate content and mechanics, ways to see how and why "water isn't always/A trickle from the eye."

Chapter 4

THE ART OF COMPOSING

Browsing among several types of texts is the fundamental must-do of modern times. No texts come first, rather diversity is displayed simultaneously (just as with the acquisition of oral language). . . . It is possible that we are witness to a new textual aesthetic, a sort of "aesthetic of fragmentation," which I still don't understand, but which I accept as a possibility. The criteria for a "well-structured text" would have to change if we accept that we are in a moment of transition.

—Emilia Ferreiro (2003), p. 51

Young writers only write as well as the parameters we set for them in terms of content and mechanics integration. And when we are highly conscious and thoughtful about these parameters, and continually adjust them to fit our goals and students' needs and talents, we direct and inspire young writers to write varied "types of texts" and to "learn that no texts come first" (Ferreiro, 2003, p. 51). We are now at an interesting juncture in teaching writing for how we define and set parameters for written texts. It's a fruitful point to reconsider the texts we set for children and expect them to compose and write, and find new ways for all young writers to access existing texts *and* create new ones. We and they need to be part of the dialogue about the "aesthetic of fragmentation" (Ferreiro, 2003, p. 51), and to re-examine the texts that "count" in our writing instruction and how we approach content and mechanics integration.

A critical piece of composing well for young writers is our unspoken and spoken desire that their writing will make a difference in their lives and ours. The editors of *The New Yorker* recently described how they selected 20 talented new young authors and what they looked for in their writing submissions.

In some cases, we saw an explanation of talent from the first chapter or story; a freshness of perspective, observation, humor, or feeling. In others, we saw a stealthier buildup of thought and linguistic innovation. Some were brilliant at doing one thing. Others made radical shifts of focus and style from one piece to the next. What was notable in all the writing, above and beyond a mastery of language and of storytelling, was a palpable sense of ambition. (*The New Yorker*, 2010, p. 50)

It is this drive and "ambition" for the process and product of composing that propels young writers to compose with a measure of confidence, drive, energy, hope, and skill. For Ken Macrorie (1984), we write well not by trying to "sound like a writer" but by trying "to tell truths and be a writer" (p. 269). For many young writers, it's our ambition and drive as educators that inspire children to have something to say and the confidence to say it well.

This is especially important for those young writers who are already too accustomed to feeling that they cannot write well. As Lisa Delpit (2002) notes, "Those of us who teach must first make our students recognize their potential brilliance" (p. 46). So much of composing well requires this belief in the "potential brilliance" of young writers—it is what inspires young writers, nurtures their composing, and pulls them along as they refine their writing over time. This belief in the brilliance of young writers is also grounded in "a commitment to the students' academic achievement, their cultural competence, and their socio-political consciousness" (Ladson-Billings, 2002, p. 112).

COMPOSING AND AUTHORSHIP

I use the term *compose* to indicate the literary and the aesthetic aspects of writing for young writers—that their writing has an external and internal beauty that emerges from a special twist or melding of content and mechanics. It is akin to the aesthetics of composing music, of continually replaying and playing anew in one's musical mind the melody or the chorus or the refrains, which eventually evolve and build into a cohesive piece or a set of pieces.

Although I've devoted separate chapters in this book to planning, composing, and revising, these three elements overlap, and the more crossover we do, the tighter the connection between the three elements.

Composing refers to everything a writer does from the time the first words are put on paper until all drafts are completed. Sometimes when a writer must rehearse by writing, there is overlap between the two, composing and rehearsing. (Graves, 1994, p. 7)

James Moffett (1988) also called for a more elevated view of writing as "full-fledged authoring" and "an authentic expression of an individual's ideas, original in the sense that he or she has synthesized them for himself or herself" (p. 76). Moffett emphasizes composing and authorship in two central ways. Writers need access to "firsthand content" from one's "feelings, fantasies, sensations, memories, and reflections" and also to "secondhand content" from "interviews, stored information, and the writing of others" (p. 76). In synthesizing combinations of "firsthand" and "secondhand" content, writers draw from their toolbox of strategies and knowledge of written language mechanics. Authors do so with care and skill because "authorship" is essentially a "focused and edited version of inner speech" (p. 76), which is the Vygotskian (1978, 1986) idea that inner speech is akin to the inner workings of the human mind.

When authors write and compose, we play with the varied cognitive, linguistic, and cultural dimensions of inner speech. Moffett (1988) advocates looking at several key dimensions of composing:

- revising inner speech (our ideas without words)
- shaping content (writing topics and forms)
- paraphrasing and summarizing (content from other texts and writers)
- transcribing and copying (integration of language from other texts and writers)
- drawing and handwriting (imagery as a sensorimotor activity)

When we compose at the level of "full-fledged authorship," according to Moffett, we are "simultaneously *drawing* [original emphasis] letters," "*transcribing*" our inner voice, "*plagiarizing* concepts" from our culture (and that of others), "*crafting*" our "thoughts into language forms," and "*revising*" our beginning ideas and feelings (p. 77) that have little or no "conventional language" attached to them. Moffett's emphasis on inner speech and levels of simultaneity form an umbrella view of composing—and one that takes in planning (from Chapter 3), composing (this chapter), and editing (Chapter 5).

Composing is also "more" than writing since "'writing' is only one piece of the puzzle that is 'composing'" (Bissex, 1996, p. 204). Composing, and composing well, takes in the range of intangibles of content and mechanics that "add up" to Moffett's "full-fledged authorship."

> Composing is the getting ready to take the risk; it's the struggling to develop an idea; it's the self-doubt, the inner critic constantly challenging you; it's all the revision that happens before you ever get a word down on paper. Composing is the thinking, the problem solving, the choices. It's the totality of every act that finally produces "writing." And this whole process is different for each one of us. (Bissex, 1996, pp. 204–205)

Composing is also about the heart and the soul, and the two-way street between composing and feeling. As the songwriter Bill Withers said about his songwriting, "I was feeling what I said" (Frere-Jones, 2010, p. 76). This counters the traditional advice to "write what you feel," and instead suggests that another process holds truth, too—composing and feelings go hand in hand.

Given the "built-in" power of composing to also include planning and revision and editing, much of the power of composing is *already* in the first draft, the first composing go-round. No matter the genre or task, the allure and the drive of composing for young writers often comes about through *moments of voice*, which take in the moods, tenor, images, words, ideas, revelations, and memories of writers as they compose. For young writers, who often can muster only so much linguistic and emotional strength in their first go-round of composing, we need to help them marshal all of their resources for the first act or draft of composing. This is what will carry them through a piece, poem, sentence, essay, report, letter, or story. We need to renew our efforts to give significance to the primacy of the first "draft" for young writers. When young children compose, much of the primacy and the immediacy of the writing are there at the beginning. Composing, like reading, is essentially drama. Samuel Coleridge, the great 18th- and 19th-century writer, spoke of this drama.

> The reader should be carried forward not merely or chiefly by the mechanical impulse of curiosity, or by a restless desire to arrive at a final solution, but the pleasurable activity of mind excited by the attractions of the journey itself. (Chapter XIV, 1985)

Much of what pulls along writers are the "attractions" of the composing journey. For young writers, then, we need to break down these "attractions" and make sure that we sprinkle these along the composing journey to entice and keep young writers going.

IDEAS AND STRATEGIES FOR COMPOSING WELL

Powerful and effective strategies for composing well take into account the range of content and mechanics elements discussed in Chapters 1, 2, and 3. This section highlights three key ways to integrate content and mechanics integration in composing:

1. the use of prompts, frames, and copying
2. increasing student awareness and reflection on the composing process
3. integrating genres and reading within composing instruction

Prompts, Frames, and Copying

Writing prompts refer to the use of a linguistic frame at the word, phrase, or sentence levels to help young writers integrate content and mechanics as they begin to compose. Examples of common frames or prompts include a sentence starter ("I went walking and saw _____") or a patterned structure ("I am _____/I like _____/I eat _____").

Caveats. Prompts and frames offer several advantages when used thoughtfully and carefully, but there are a few caveats to keep in mind.

1. Prompts and frames can become redundant and dull if overused and young writers come to expect that composing is *only* the use of prompts and frames, which it is not.
2. If used too often, prompts can inhibit the acquisition of new and varied vocabulary and syntactical structures for new language learners.
3. Prompts and frames can inhibit young writers from thinking and feeling on their own to come up with topics and ideas for their writing.
4. Prompts and frames can become too closely aligned with writing assessments, confusing assessment with teaching for young writers.
5. Since they are teacher-created and contain correct mechanics, prompts and frames can prove a daunting model of mechanics for some young writers who balk at emulating or continuing the prompt or frame.

Benefits. On the other hand, prompts and frames offer young writers several benefits.

1. They offer children a "first learning place" to start and something to go on for composing. They also offer us our own "first teaching place" to start off a group of children in their composing.
2. Prompts and frames, when well used, benefit new language learners by providing an inside-out approach focused on language chunks (Gregory, 2008). They can serve to "control" the amount of vocabulary and complexity of syntax so that new language learners are afforded an effective developmental progression for their composing.
3. Prompts and frames can mimic or incorporate elements of oral and written texts that provide new language learners with "just enough" recognizable and patterned language and content for

starting to compose. They provide young writers with elements of the outside-in approach (Gregory, 2008), featuring large chunks of language from stories and other texts.

4. They support new language learners and other children who are not yet steeped in mainstream cultural and linguistic expectations and who thus benefit from a teacher-supported format or structure for composing well. A number of these students (and their families) "may expect teachers to provide direct and explicit instruction" (Reyes, 1992, p. 430), and frames and prompts can provide a strong teacher model for integrating content and mechanics for successful composing. In this way, prompts and frames can complement the idea of children creating and discovering their own writing topics and become "an appropriate adaptation that will increase" the "likelihood of success with diverse learners" (Reyes, 1992, p. 440).

5. Prompts and frames can strengthen and support children's reading, providing a parallel literacy experience in composing and using key vocabulary or syntactical structures from their reading texts.

Value for the Composing of New Language Learners. Florence Tse, in her kindergarten class of mostly new language learners, uses elements of sentence frames at the beginning of the year. She also plans out a series of steps that ensure a "gradual release of responsibility" (Miller, 2002) from her teacher modeling and increase her students' composing independence over the course of the year. Florence's emphasis on teacher modeling and chunking of language into bite-size pieces provides a comfortable foundation for her students to begin composing. Since her students are "pretty nonverbal in English," they need direct support and guidance in "having their ideas stated" in writing.

Florence likes to use storybooks and texts with predictable syntactical patterns and engaging content to help her students compose.

> I listen to a lot of their conversations during turn and talk or at the lunch table. Sometimes their conversations are addressed to me, but sometimes they are shared between friends. They're good jumping points for me to see where our writing can go and where they would be the most successful. In one conversation, we were talking about how we're really in love with books. We had read *I Went Walking* by Sue Williams (1996), which the children loved. They took that book and actually made their own sentence frame and made their own books from it.

In another example of using predictable and bite-size text from a book to help her students learn to compose, Florence had read *I Will Not Ever Eat a Tomato* (Child, 2000) as a read-aloud, and her students discussed their food memories and what they liked and didn't like to eat. One child was particularly taken with the book and wanted to write about it. So she looked at the cover and wrote out seven blank lines for the words in the title, and then wrote down "I" and "a," which was "as much as she could write." She then brought her paper to Florence for help, and Florence wrote the rest of the title. In this example, the format of the blank lines is combined with copying from a text, and both elements help young new language learners begin to compose.

Florence then extends the frames to incorporate sight words from the children's reading texts. Florence also provides a sentence on paper. Her students cut it out, rearrange it into a sentence, copy it in their own writing, and then draw a picture for it. Over time, this activity helps her students with vocabulary understanding, recognizing sight words, letter formation, spelling sight words, letter formation, and connecting text to picture.

In the next step, around November, Florence writes out a question that she reads with her students, and then they discuss possible answers and the children draw pictures to respond to the question. Later, by January, the children draw and write their own responses to Florence's question. Florence circulates around the room as children draw, directly helping the children find a "jumping-off point" for their written responses. She also encourages children to use "peer support to spell words out, especially if they know that a friend can help them sound out a word better than they can." Sometimes her students have some "sentence sense" about the syntactical structures they wish to compose, and Florence encourages these children to go ahead with their composing, while she directly supports other young writers who need more support with forming syntactical structures in English. If needed, Florence talks with her students in Cantonese to help them understand what they want to write and how they will write it.

> I want their ideas to be fluid, to flow, and so sometimes I translate some of their ideas from Cantonese to English. So they're describing their picture in Cantonese to me and I help them with the words. I say, "These are the words for it in English." This is all on a one-on-one basis.

As her students gain confidence and skill as the year progresses, Florence even sees a regression in her students' control and mastery over mechanics.

> Sometimes the message is so important to the children that they forget all the rules for conveying their message in print. I see this more at

about this time of year (February). At first, my students are very careful and very cautious about how they're writing their sentence. Now they have really good ideas and as they're writing they're using less conventional spellings. For instance, they know a sight word and they're not writing the sight word we've learned, such as writing "lik" instead of "like."

Stacia Stribling and Susan Kraus (2007) noticed a similar developmental regression in the writing of their 1st-grade students.

> While we were excited about the increasing depth of the children's stories, we were troubled by their "disregard" for the writing conventions we had been teaching. We were torn between celebrating children's passion for writing compelling stories and worrying about their inability to consistently use proper mechanics . . . the children could not hold these two concepts—interesting storyline and proper writing conventions—in their minds at the same time. There appeared to be a cognitive overload. (p. 13)

This back and forth of inverting the content/mechanics ratio also recalls Marie Clay's (1975) observation that children's early writing knowledge can be so specific that one new insight or discovery can change "the child's perception of the entire system drastically, or may even disorganize it" (p. 15). Later in the year, Florence's students slip "in terms of mechanics but go further in terms of their ideas" for writing and are "more ready to share their writing." Still later in the year, when her students write more than one draft, Florence tapes their multiple drafts to the back of their final draft and can see that her students do return their attention to mechanics.

BRINGING AWARENESS TO THE COMPOSING PROCESS

Amanda Abarbanel-Rice emphasizes self-monitoring and reflection to promote powerful composing for her 2nd-graders. Amanda's composing strategies echo Emilia Ferreiro's (2003) praise for the value of reflection and awareness of written content and mechanics.

> But when they [children] try to understand writing they must objectify speaking, that is, they must turn it into an object of reflection: to discover that it has parts that can be ordered, interchanged, classified; to discover that similarities and differences in signifiers are not parallel to similarities and differences in meaning; to discover that there are many ways of "saying the same thing" in speaking and writing; to construct a "metalanguage" for speaking about language, now converted into an object of thought. (Ferreiro, 2003, p. 73)

Believing that her 2nd-graders are capable of this developmental leap toward Ferreiro's "converting" language into "an object of thought," Amanda continually asks her students to reflect and think about the forms and functions of writing and composing.

- Writing is hard because you have to concentrate. (Haley)
- Writers write stories about their lives, made-up stories. (Bianca)
- You have to be very focused so you can get a lot of writing down. (Camerah)
- You can make a story with your family. (Luis)
- Writing is hard because when writers are done, they have just begun. When you are done you have to edit. (Audrey)
- When a writer thinks they are done, it's not true. They are at the beginning. Before you edit and add punctuation, you have to reread it and add details that aren't there before. (Benji)

Amanda's composing philosophy and strategies integrate an emphasis on reflection with a focus on accuracy in mechanics and engaging content.

Over the year, our writing covers mental images, a how-to genre, literature study and writing stories in the style of an author, an insect study that is a huge nonfiction writing project, personal narratives, poetry, biography writing, and a lot of writing in math. When they are doing this writing, I am also reading to my students from that genre through read-alouds. I'm also trying to have their early guided reading books also be from that genre. I want them to increase their familiarity of each genre from both sides—reading and writing.

Amanda also uses three specific ways to foster reflection:

1. talking to her students about the art of composing
2. focusing on mental images and visualization
3. using specialized language from her writing, the students' writing, and published texts

These composing strategies help young writers gain access to what James Gray (2000) called "secrets of style" (p. 40), or knowledge of form so "students can take in the possibilities [of form and style] and use them to say confidently what they wanted to say" (p. 40). Amanda also follows Lucy Calkins's (1986) insight that "authorship does not begin with the struggle to put something big into print; rather, it begins with living with a sense of awareness" (p. 3).

Amanda first steeps her composing instruction in a writing philosophy that sees composing as embodying a back and forth dance between content and mechanics.

> It's hard to integrate content and mechanics; sometimes the emphasis is more on one, and sometimes it's more on the other. The notion that once you put that pencil down, you're not actually done, is hard for us and for young writers to see. It's really the writer's process, and integrating content and mechanics is part of this process. You have to persist, and older writers—2nd-graders are just at the beginning of this—they learn that when they do go back and read for content and add more, their writing gets better. Second grade is the first year that they are having this experience of seeing their writing getting better. I try to bring awareness to this process, to have them see that it was so hard for you [a student]—you worked so hard and you kept going back and you wanted to be done and you weren't done yet—and look at how good this last piece of writing is. It's so much better now than it was at first, and maybe you are articulating a point more (which is more content) or maybe it's more readable to your audience (which is more mechanics). If there is no audience, it would not matter if it were legible or not. It needs to be legible to young writers themselves because they can't edit and change the content if they can't reread their own writing.

Amanda emphasizes self-monitoring and revisiting texts "all the time, no matter what kind of writing it is." Amanda continually tells her students, "When a writer's done, she or he has just begun." When Amanda asks her students at the end of the year what they learned about writing, they "often talk about how hard writing is and how much effort they have to do in writing. So many of them quote the saying 'when a writer's done, she or he has just begun,' and I think that it really strikes a chord for them."

Second, in her mini-lessons and as Amanda works with students as they compose, she emphasizes the power of images and visualization for powerful composing.

> Good readers make mental images, and they just don't make mental images visually, they also get images from hearing sounds, feeling texture, smelling something, or tasting. The writer is using all of these senses just as in reading. A good writer evokes all that for the reader. I do a lot of that throughout the year and have my students experience what mental images are from the reader's and the writer's perspective. I've played around with the phrase "mental image" because I'm still not sure

whether this is the language that works best for children, and I've asked them what works best and they don't have one term. Sometimes they like "picture in their head" and sometimes "picture in your imagination." I haven't found one phrase that covers it for all students.

Amanda's emphasis on mental images for composing has its roots in the power of visualizing for effective reading (Miller, 2002), and Amanda directly guides her students to make the transfer back and forth between breaking down texts (reading) and building up texts (composing and writing).

> They get an image in their mind, sketch it, and then write it. They reread it and see if there was anything in their sketch that they did not get into their writing. Then they add more detail and inevitably there is something they missed. They read it to someone else and that person's comments are what they can picture in their head. They go back from that conference and add something else. Their goal is communicating their mental image. I limit it to two changes. It's a short piece. They literally cut out the changes and tape them on. They add their two or three more sentences, and they tape on the next part. So I first do a mini-lesson on "When a writer is done, he or she has just begun" and then one on mental images. I then do many mini-lessons on a range of mechanics as we go back and edit our mental image writing for capitals, punctuation, and spelling. For the moment, that particular piece of writing is done. At that point, I've carried them through the entire writing process relatively quickly; each person's writing probably did only two changes. They may have added one more sentence for a detail and they fixed their capitals.

Amanda's foundation of visualization and images promotes content and mechanics integration for her students as they experience the entire composing process.

> What is my goal for my 2nd-graders? Do I want them to write a 6-week piece that is really, really polished? Or do I want them to experience the *full* writing process? I think that's what I want—to know experientially how to construct their knowledge and all the parts of the writing process so they really understand it. This is their first time. And it ends with publishing and reading to an audience, whether it's their peers or a kindergarten or 1st-grade class or their families.

This emphasis on composing as *experience* recalls John Dixon's (1967) observation that "certainty about language is in a sense certainty about experience" (p. 9). In other words, young writers gain confidence and skill in composing through meaningful writing experiences with others.

Third, Amanda uses specialized academic language to give her students the terminology, strategies, and a sequence for improving their composing and content/mechanics integration.

> For content, I think of elements of writing and what is good writing. I include voice, luscious language or attention to language and vocabulary, the whole notion of the drawing out of small moments, and how the teaching of reading and the teaching of writing are connected. The whole notion of metaphor and simile, which is connected to mental images, is something that I emphasize, too. We focus on certain words, we learn what they mean, and we work on synonyms and antonyms. I choose words from our reading and I read the words from the books where I found them. The students talk to each other and they write phrases for what it means—synonyms, antonyms, and sample sentences and often a picture. Even in the sample sentences, there is content; I'll point out that in phrases you don't need capitalization or punctuation so we can focus on vocabulary. This helps with academic language and helps students with less experience with writing and English language learners (ELLs). I believe that good writers are using words on purpose for a specific meaning. It's not so simple; you just don't have to read a lot to expand your vocabulary—you actually have to pay more attention to writing as you compose. The mechanics involves learning these words, and the content involves using these words to make our meaning more specific, more vibrant, and more comprehensible to our readers. This is particularly important for English learners and children with less writing experience; they really benefit from attention to word meaning and word choice in their writing.

Amanda takes examples of "luscious language" (phrases and sentences that evoke strong images and senses), "wonderful words" (words that move along a story or engage the reader), and "strong leads" (effective beginning hooks) from her students' writing, her own, her read-alouds, and the children's independent reading texts to model possible content and mechanics integration for her students' composing.

For example, Amanda and her students brainstormed instances of luscious language in Jane Yolen's (1987) *Owl Moon*:

- The trees stood as still as giant statues.
- Train whistle was long and low like a sad sad song.

- Someone's icy hand was palm-down on my back.
- I was a shadow.
- When you go owling you don't need real words.

Amanda and her students found more in other texts:

- Danny is like a giant bowling ball!
- The candy centers were as white as snow.
- The cocoa was as thick and rich as melted chocolate bars.
- The train thundered through the quiet wilderness.
- A blinding flash lit up the woods with a blue-green light.

The practice of identifying luscious language integrates Eve Gregory's (2008) inside-out (individual words and phrases) and outside-in approaches (larger chunks of texts). For example, in Jane Yolen's (1986) line, "When you go owling you don't need real words," the content idea of experiencing something magical is rendered to the reader with the simple and yet telling phrase, "you don't need real words" (p. 29).

Amanda and her students also look for "wonderful words" in their writing. They make a list as they go, gathering examples from their writing and reading texts:

- Bolted
- tremendous tug
- banging pot
- claw like hands
- lean wolves
- sparkling crystal
- smooth shiny surf
- boiling brown lake

Amanda's attention to luscious language and wonderful words helps students with elements of mechanics such as writing a strong lead to a piece. It gives her students chunks of language (words, phrases, sentences) to keep in mind *while* reading and writing effective larger elements of composing.

For example, her students found strong leads in their independent reading books, wrote them down on paper, and Amanda and the students discussed how the content and mechanics went together to create a strong and effective lead.

- Before Bean met Ivy, she didn't like her. (Blackal & Burrows, 2007, *Ivy and Bean*, p. 1)

- Mr. Watson and Mrs. Watson have a pig named Mercer. (DiCamillo, 2009, *Mercy Watson*, p. 1)
- Chester had his own way of doing things. (Henkes, 1997, *Chester's Way*, p. 1)
- If you don't have any friends, follow these simple instructions: . . . (Carlson, 1994, *How to Lose All Your Friends*, p. 1)
- There once lived a wolf who loved to eat more than anything else in the world. (Kasza, 1996, *The Wolf's Chicken Stew*, p. 1)

The attention to strong leads provides students with an integration of content and mechanics in *one* sentence, and an important sentence that leads off a story or other kind of text. By selecting only one sentence, young writers can search for a bite-size and manageable amount of language to consider using in their own composing.

Amanda also integrates mini-lessons during the composing process to highlight particular elements of content and mechanics.

> Some students compose without any editing, without any organization or any notion of their focus or goal. So I need to stop and give mini-lessons to help organize their writing. For example, I say, "OK, you've only done dialogue. Let's talk about the strengths of dialogue, the mechanics of dialogue, variations of using and not using dialogue." In narrative writing, I also focus on mechanics such as dialogue, action, setting, character, problem/solution/climax, strong beginnings, strong endings. In nonfiction, I have a unit that the children love, and I teach the elements of nonfiction. These can be taught as an element of mechanics, though if it's too isolated it becomes really dry. It needs to be taught in the context of students' writing.

Amanda takes advantage of the potential to stop and start the composing process, and slips in structured attention to certain elements of content and mechanics in ways that connect to what and how her students are writing at a particular moment.

James Britton (1970) discussed the potential of composing to help us reflect on what, how, and why we are writing.

> But it seems to me that the differences that exist between the *process* of speaking and the *process* of writing are more relevant to our concerns here. And the most important of these lies in the fact that writing allows more time for premeditation; there is a gap between the forging of the utterance and its reception. Because of this premeditation, because we can work on the writing until we are satisfied with it, I think that the shaping process is a sharper one than it is in talking. (p. 30)

Amanda's attention to elements of powerful composing such as luscious language, wonderful words, and strong leads all allow for Britton's "time for premeditation" and a "sharpening" of the "shaping process" to integrate content and mechanics.

INTEGRATING GENRES ACROSS THE COMPOSING CURRICULUM

Madhuvanti Khare also uses varied writing genres to maximize content and mechanics integration in her 3rd-grade composing curriculum. Madhuvanti uses Lucy Calkins's *Firsthand* curriculum (2003), her own strategies and ideas, and three grade-level writing prompts (fall, winter, spring) used in her district.

Madhuvanti crafts a developmentally appropriate sequence of writing genres that helps her students meld content and mechanics in their writing:

- poetry and/or personal memoir (September and October)
- district letter-writing prompt (mid-September)
- publish memoir piece (end of October)
- fables (October and November)
- folktales and fairy tales (December)
- realistic fiction (December and January)
- district realistic fiction prompt (February)
- biography (March)
- science research reports (April to June)
- district summary writing prompt (May)

Madhuvanti's composing genres complement and build on each other. For example, Madhuvanti uses the district's letter-writing prompt early in the year to introduce paragraph writing, which she revisits later on in the year.

> I know the writing prompts well enough [she was the lead writer on the grade 3 prompts] to feel comfortable that they're things that students need to learn and the sequence in which they need to learn them. It's nice to start off thinking about paragraphs early in the year because by the end of the year in my class, I move into five-paragraph essays. For the first prompt, they have to write a letter to their new teacher, telling me about themselves. So we start working on the mechanics of paragraph indenting and topic sentence and supporting details since that particular prompt asks for one or two paragraphs. I show the class about paragraphs and letters and we practice during literacy centers and during our writing time.

Madhuvanti's planning allows her students to compose in one genre more than once over the year, and for content and mechanics integration to build and merge. For instance, the one- or two-paragraph letter early in the year is a developmental precursor to multi-paragraph essays later in the year. Madhuvanti's curriculum thus creates *long* and *elastic* zones of proximal development for composing, as seen in the trail for paragraph writing that starts at the beginning of the year and carries on until the end of the year.

Composing Routines

Adapting a classic writer's workshop format (Atwell, 1987; Calkins, 1986, 2006; Graves, 1983, 1994), Madhuvanti has a daily 45- to 50-minute writing period. She usually has a 5- to 10-minute mini-lesson, the class then writes for 40 minutes as she talks with individual students and pauses for a mid-session teaching point, and then concludes with a short sharing session. After a month of getting to know her students and their writing, Madhuvanti puts her students in pairs for reading and responding to each other's writing as they compose. Madhuvanti believes that "when they read each other's work they can talk about what works and what doesn't and the feedback comes from a different perspective than their own."

Madhuvanti's composing sessions emphasize sharing and group collaboration. Her mini-lessons often involve having her students sit with their writing partners on the rug. The partners bring their writing journals and, after a mini-lesson, the partners often write something short and then share it with their partner. After another 20 minutes of composing on the rug or at their desks, Madhuvanti does a mid-workshop teaching point.

> If there is something someone's taken on that we talked about earlier or we were writing about "how do you come up with a good title" and somebody came up with a good title—it's just a brief pause, as I say, "Oh, you know we were talking about this earlier, everybody look at what Johnny did"—and they go back to writing.

As she converses one-on-one with students, Madhuvanti selects and informs a few students that they will share part of their writing at the end of the workshop.

> I think the strongest way to know that a piece is good is to have students share them. So every day during writing time, depending on what the day's mini-lesson focused on, I try to find two or three examples from the students who worked on that focus during writing time that day. For example, if our focus involved using quotation

marks and having some interesting dialogue, I'll have them share just a sentence or two or three out loud at the end of writing time so that the class can hear it. Since I am doing the choosing, I tend to choose the stuff that's successful rather than unsuccessful, so that the class can start hearing what it sounds like in their language, too. So it's not necessarily all of Sandra Cisneros or whoever we've been reading at the time.

By looking for evidence of strong examples of content and mechanics, Madhuvanti uses the students' writing to circle back and reinforce the topic of the day's mini-lesson. Asking students to only share a few sentences is an economical way to focus on content and mechanics.

Reading Just Ahead

Like Amanda, Madhuvanti uses her read-alouds of high-quality literature and nonfiction to read *just ahead* of the next composing genre. This helps students compose in four important ways.

First, it builds anticipation and helps students predict particular elements of content and mechanics for a certain genre. This echoes James Britton's (1982) idea of "shaping at the point of utterance" both for oral and written language (p. 141).

> I want to associate spontaneous shaping, whether in speech or writing, with the moment by moment interpretive process by which we make sense of what is happening around us; to see each as an instance of the pattern-forming propensity of man's mental processes. Thus, when we come to write, what is delivered to the pen is in part already shaped, stamped with the image of our own ways of perceiving. But the intention to share, inherent in spontaneous utterance, sets up a demand for further shaping. (p. 141)

Madhuvanti's reading just ahead of the next genre stretches out the range of young writers' ZPDs to make room for Britton's "shaping at the point of utterance." It helps young writers shape and integrate *what* they might write (their potential content) with *how* they might write (their potential mechanics) *while* they are finishing composing in one genre and *before* composing in the next. Britton also viewed the "developed writing process as one of hearing an inner voice dictating forms of the written language appropriate to the task at hand" (p. 144). Madhuvanti's reading ahead of the next genre gives her students a sneak preview and gets their "inner voices" attuned to elements of content and mechanics ("forms of the written language") in a particular genre.

Second, reading just ahead of the next genre benefits new language learners as it focuses their attention on content and mechanics through their receptive language (listening to the read-alouds), productive language (discussing and talking about the text elements), and visual recognition (pictures and visuals in the texts). This process allows Madhuvanti to break down elements of mechanics and content in reading and link them to writing, a critical process for new language learners. It is also an example of what María de la luz Reyes (1992) calls an "appropriate adaptation" for linguistically diverse learners by directly pointing out mechanics and content integration in the read-alouds. Madhuvanti links content and mechanics *across* and *within* genres, and holds onto her role "as a mediator of knowledge," highlighting "the importance of form" (Reyes, 1992, p. 443) for her students.

Third, reading just ahead further helps new language learners preview elements of powerful writing *before* they are actually composing. As Lucy Calkins (1986) observes, "Once they have written a full draft, they will have time for editing, but during composition, concern about correctness competes with the more timely concern about content, word choice, voice, tone, and rhythm" (p. 198). Madhuvanti's reading just ahead gives new language learners time ahead of composing to listen for, consider, and understand an author's and an entire genre's particular "content, word choice, voice, tone, and rhythm."

Fourth, reading ahead into the next genre while still composing in the current genre instills a sense of power and knowledge for young writers. Emilia Ferreiro (2003) observes how young writers who are immersed in joyful writing experiences focus on essential forms and functions of writing, and are more likely to believe they have something to say. They may still have errors in mechanics (spacing, punctuation, spelling), but their writing has story language, narrative rhythm, and knowledge of how to "organize" what they want to write (Ferreiro, 2003, p. 30). Conversely, young writers who are not immersed in read-alouds, rich reading experiences, and sophisticated and supportive writing experiences too often only experience writing as a focus "on letters, syllables, and isolated words" (p. 33). Madhuvanti's reading ahead, and her discussions and brainstorming about cross-genre content and mechanics, ensure that her students access varied "text types" and are reading and listening "critically" (p. 51) as the building blocks for effective composing.

Reading-to-Writing Transfer

Madhuvanti mixes and matches longer chapter books with shorter picture books to promote a reading-to-writing transfer that models content and mechanics integration in composing.

> We're usually doing longer chapter book read-alouds from the beginning of the year but also shorter picture books in realistic fiction so that students also get the idea they can write shorter stories. At 3rd grade, they get very ambitious and want to start writing chapter books, [which gets] boring, and so being able to really show them that a short story—that has a good character development and a good plot line—is going to be a lot more effective. I think the shorter form definitely does improve the content. I teach this way because if you read enough of these stories that go on and on and on and really go nowhere, you realize that if you could just cut out 60% of it, they'd have a story in there someplace.

Using picture books provides developmentally appropriate and bite-size elements of Eve Gregory's (2008) outside-in approach: story structure (beginning, middle, end), story language (metaphor, simile, onomatopoeia), chunking of story language (formulaic story starters and endings), universal truths and morals (content), and written language clues (semantic, syntactic, bibliographic, lexical, grapho-phonic) (p. 184). In terms of semantics, storybooks also "introduce children to different ways of life, to new experiences and cultural practices" and yet "draw upon universal morals and values" (p. 187). In terms of syntactical development, stories "provide difficult yet memorable chunks of language which are often reinforced by rhymes and repetition" (p. 187).

Madhuvanti uses a range of strategies to promote her students' evolving orchestration of these outside-in elements.

> For composing personal narrative and realistic fiction, I use Lucy Calkins's idea of a story mountain. This year, I had my students write their plot points on seven Post-its and I said, "This is what you've got to tell your story." The nice thing with giving them about seven Post-its is that they can always negotiate with me if they feel like they need more. It prevents them from having a story that goes on and on, and gives them an outline that they can easily pull off the Post-it and put in their journal so they can see what they're working on and how long it takes. We also talk about how each plot point for a short story shouldn't take more than half a page. It's all approximate, but young writers like to know how much. So how much do I have to write today? It helps them quantify their writing. And for those students who do go on and on, it gives them a way to rein themselves in.

The Post-its are visuals that can include writing and sketches, harkening back to younger children's earliest attempts at writing through drawing.

I link reading and writing as much as I can visually. It helps our struggling students and the English learners. For example, using a story
mountain visual and really reading picture books and plotting out the
story based on what we've read together links reading and writing,
and so I say, "This author had to think about his or her story before
they wrote it and now we're going to think about our stories before
we write them." I do as much visual representation with the whole
class as I can.

In late January, Madhuvanti read Alma Flor Ada's (1995) *My Name Is
María Isabel* to the class as a model of realistic fiction. María Isabel Salazar
López is 9 years old when her family has to move 2 months into the school
year, and she is forced to attend a new school. Arriving in her new class-
room, her new teacher says, "Ah, María Lopez . . . we already have two
Marías in this class. Why don't we call you Mary instead?" (p. 8).

As Madhuvanti read and discussed the book's early plot points and
other elements of realistic fiction, Madhuvanti and the class recorded their
emerging ideas on Post-its that she kept on the board behind the class rug.

> *Madhuvanti:* In terms of our story mountain for *My Name Is María
> Isabel*, where are we? We're kind of right here. (points to middle
> Post-it) Do we know what the problem is? (waits) It's part of a
> bigger problem.
> *Derrick:* Things aren't going too well.
> *Madhuvanti:* Yes, Isabel is having a hard time adjusting to her new
> school. What's recess like for a new child? Alma, you were new
> last year. What was it like?
> *Alma:* It was scary.
> *Elijah:* I was scared on my first day.
> *Madhuvanti:* What do you do when you're nervous when you're
> new?
> *Alma:* I'd go up to some girls and say, "Hi."
> *Tanica:* I got brave and asked someone to play.
> *Rasheed:* I made conversations. (Madhuvanti and the class continue
> to talk about what it's like to be new at a school. Madhuvanti
> then continues to read from Chapter 3, "Recess," where, outside
> on the playground, a girl named Marta invites María to play
> jump rope.)
> *Madhuvanti:* (pausing) Those of you using a lot of dialogue in your
> stories, listen to this: "'Come on, let's go jump rope,' Marta said,
> tugging on María Isabel's arm. María Isabel hesitated, and Marta
> tugged again. 'Come on,' she urged.'" (p. 14) Who has a picture

of what that might feel like, for María to be led by hand and
"tugged" by Marta?

Lila: It might be startling.

Madhuvanti: Yes, it might be. (continues reading, "The rhythm of the
jump rope as it brushed against the ground was soothing. It reminded María Isabel of her grandmother Chabela's rocking chair,
the one her grandmother would rock her to sleep in, or of the ebb
and flow of the waves in front of her grandfather Antonio's house
(p. 14)." How many of you have heard the term *ebb and flow*?
Who's ever watched the tide? That's what it means, the tide going
in and out. (reads on), "María Isabel loved that beach. She loved
to go out for a walk early in the morning, picking up treasures
the sea had left behind the night before; shells that looked like
mother-of-pearl; bits of white coral; maybe even a sand dollar or
two" (p. 16).

Ahmed: What's a sand dollar?

Madhuvanti: They're a sea creature. When they wash up on shore,
you can see the creature's breathing holes. (Continues to read.)
Why was the author taking us to the waves after we were at the
jump roping? Is it OK to add side stories? Yes, as long as they're
connected. (Reads the next section, where María has fallen because she was daydreaming, and as the girls return to the classroom María thinks to herself, "Tomorrow, when her knee didn't
hurt so much, she would show them how well she could jump"
[p. 16]. Madhuvanti points to the story mountain Post-its behind
her.) We're still pretty early in the story mountain. The author is
taking her time to get into the problem of the story. Listen to how
Alma Flor Ada gives you, the reader, time to get into the problem
of the story. So today when you work with your writing partners,
ask each other if the problems in your stories are stretched out,
so as authors you are not rushing to solve your story's problem.
(The children then go to their desks and the partners explain
where they were in their written stories, and they give their
opinions about where the composing might go that day in terms
of stretching out the problem. Some children comment *as* their
partner starts to write, reading their partner's text as they write
and listening to their partner say what they are writing at the
moment.)

This teaching sequence features a read-aloud, Post-its as a visual, attention
to vocabulary and syntax, open discussion with the class, reference to the
author's goals and strategies, and direct linking to the children's current

writing, all of which promote a strong reading-to-writing transfer. By doing so, Madhuvanti tightens the content and mechanics connections for her students, showing how they are linked in the read-aloud text and how they can be linked in the students' current composing projects. Madhuvanti also integrates Eve Gregory's (2008) outside-in (using the story read-aloud to focus on content, story form, character, problem/solution) and inside-out approaches (attention to individual words, phrases, word meanings, dialogue) within the context of read-alouds and the children's writing.

When you are writing a small moment, you make it into a big piece of writing. You think of something special, and you write a lot.

—Camerah, 2nd-grader

Composing for young writers is a process of moving toward a "well-structured text" (Ferreiro, 2003). It is a process constantly in transition, as the forms and functions of written texts change both from outside and from within. The teachers featured in this chapter constantly juggle the texts that young writers need to know—the texts from oral language, books, our writing, their writing—so that they are continually moving toward a tightening of content and mechanics, a happy pairing of the two.

We need to believe in the "potential brilliance" (Delpit, 2002) of young writers and engage in "full-fledged authoring" (Moffett, 1988). Neither a plethora of worksheets on written language mechanics nor open-ended opportunities to write whatever comes to mind move young writers along this hoped-for path of authorship. Rather, we need what the teachers in this chapter advocate and do. Florence supports her new language learners through a sensitive and measured mix of chunks of language as linked to engaging and inviting text. Amanda emphasizes self-reflection and awareness of the challenges and joys of composing. Madhuvanti plans a thoughtful year-long curriculum, focuses on genre and form, and links reading and writing. These ideas and strategies help move content and mechanics closer together for young writers as they compose, and as they slowly build an inner sense that they can and will write "well-structured texts."

Chapter 5

EDITING AND REVISING

When you ain't talking, you put in a period.
—1st-grader

The process of editing and revising is intimately related to planning and composing. Editing and revising are not the third and final phase or sequential steps in effective content and mechanics integration for young writers. Rather, elements of editing and revision are sprinkled all along the journey of content and mechanics integration. I define editing and revising in two basic ways, and expand and deepen these definitions in this chapter. Editing is attention to changes in small units of mechanics and content (word choice, punctuation, spelling, syntax, flow, length, appearance). Revision is attention to changes in larger units of mechanics and content (a feeling, an idea, a piece of information, part of a format or structure, part of a genre).

CHALLENGES

Editing and revising pose particular challenges for young writers and for ourselves as teachers of writing.

For Young Writers

Editing and *revising* are often two terms that young writers are least likely to want to hear. They can prove a disincentive for young writers for several reasons:

- Children are physically tired and lack the energy to go back and revise (this can apply to kindergartners as well as 4th-graders).
- They're too "tired" emotionally to revisit a piece and revise and edit (they've already found it a trying process to find, place, and phrase their content in a satisfactory way).

- It is too challenging spatially to go back over a text and visually find where and how to make edits and revisions—this is "the mechanics of data insertion and the aesthetics attendant to this act" (Graves, 1983, p. 155).
- They're just learning to understand basic differences between oral and written language forms and functions due to their development and/or language proficiencies. "Children at this stage are often puzzled if asked to revise a text they treat more as a 'spoken' document than a written one" (Graves, 1994, p. 278).
- Children may need additional support to make the leap from their familiar forms of oral and written language to less familiar, more "school-based" forms (syntax, word choice, tone, style, format).
- Young writers may feel as though they are being asked to go back and revise when they feel they are already done and have nothing left to say.
- Children may feel they are being asked to revise when they don't really know much about their topic. "If children are asked to revise pieces when they know little about the subject, they have little personal investment in their writing" (Graves, 1994, p. 278).
- It's too hard for young writers to reread their writing because it's too difficult to read back their own spelling and/or interpret their own handwriting.
- Children may have difficulty understanding how to use various revision or editing tools and resources (e.g., editing checklist, dictionary, personal dictionary, thesaurus, word wall).
- Children may not want to share their writing with peers and adults (due to shyness, language proficiency, and other factors) in peer and teacher conferences and whole-class sharing sessions.
- New language learners may not have sufficient linguistic knowledge and fluency (especially word meanings and syntax) to make informed editing and revising decisions.
- Young writers may want everything to be so perfect and correct that they over-emphasize mechanics at the expense of content revision.

For Ourselves as Teachers of Writing

For us, teaching revision and editing can be challenging for several reasons:

- We may need more knowledge about helping young writers go back and forth between their familiar ways of using language and "mainstream" forms of written communication.

- It may be hard to match our whole-class expectations for revision and editing with each child's particular talents and needs.
- It's challenging to find the time to help students in need of frequent one-on-one assistance with editing and revising.
- Our editing and revising tools may prove more complicated and demanding than the actual linguistic and cognitive demands of editing and revising for students.
- It can be difficult to figure out how to integrate and slip in editing and revising when children plan and compose.
- It can be a challenge deciding when and how to emphasize content and/or mechanics for the whole class and for particular children.
- In our role as editor in chief, it can be a struggle understanding how much to edit and revise for a particular young writer.
- Finding a good link between editing and revision and our writing assessment measures can be challenging.
- We may have trouble observing and understanding how much knowledge our young writers actually have about what to edit and how.
- In order to show parents and administrators that we are teaching well, we may spend too much attention on mechanics correction.
- We face the overall challenge of knowing what effective revision and editing look like, and how they apply to grade-level expectations.

It is valuable for us to recognize the challenges for young writers and for ourselves because they help us shape our revising and editing philosophy and strategies. Editing and revision are the glue that give shape and substance to a well-written piece and to an evolving body of well-formed writing. They are present all along the way as young writers write, and they touch on the most powerful and fundamental aspects of writing well.

THEORETICAL FOUNDATIONS

How we see editing and revising is also linked to our views on how and why children learn literacy, and how we view and implement content and mechanics integration in their writing. There are several key ideas that help us formulate a deeper sense of the role of editing and revision in promoting content and mechanics integration.

Internal/External

Taking a Vygotskian (1978, 1986) view of language and thought, editing and revision occur internally (internal speech) and externally (speech for others).

When young writers reflect on their writing and drawing as they plan and compose, they engage in an internal to external and back again cycle. This happens at two levels. First, young writers internally construct and engage with a written text or drawing internally (thinking ideas, feeling a feeling or sensation, or having a wordless image) and externally (trying to render some aspect of the idea, feeling, sensation, image). This level of revision mainly happens when young writers compose and give shape and substance (mechanics and content) to their writing and/or drawing. Second, and this is a slightly more advanced level, young writers resee and revise a more complete or well-shaped text internally (thinking back to where they started, where they went, and where they are now) and externally (responding to the text at hand and how/why they could change/add/delete/extend to move it in a new direction).

What's the role of content and mechanics at both levels? At both levels, young writers shape their writing/drawing to meld a certain degree of synchronization of content and mechanics. They shape it toward a melding of its internal beauty (e.g., how a character "lives" with interest and originality inside a story) and its external beauty (the look or feel or structure of the story due to the orchestration of its mechanics). The more we sense and see the degree to which young writers want to move toward this integration, the more we can reach into our editing and revision toolbox to help them move in this direction.

Premeditation and Reflection

James Britton (1970) viewed premeditation and reflection as essential for linking thought and language in revision and editing. Premeditation involves a back and forth in thought and language.

> In fact the process of writing as we normally practice it seems to be kind of a switchback. We continually read back to what we have just written, and so get into the channel again in order to go forward and write the next piece. This seems part revision, part planning, at a level of fine detail. Perhaps this constitutes the primary way in which writing differs from speaking, the primary way in which we use the premeditation that enters into writing. (p. 35)

Written language has a "constancy" "grafted" upon the "immediacy" of spoken language that "enables a speaker to reflect upon meanings" and gain "a critical awareness of his/her own thought processes" (1987, p. 23). At the surface level, which is what young writers attend to, editing and revision involve integrating content and mechanics to strengthen writing. At the foundational level, revision is about strengthening the underlying linguistic/cognitive/social talents and strategies of young writers to help them see and hear and feel more at the surface level.

The Young Writer as an Individual

For Britton (1970), young writers are individual learners who "read back" and "go forward" at two levels. First is the level *within* a piece of writing. Second is the level between and *across* pieces of writing. For example, in Chapter 3, I talked about how Rickey, a kindergartner, used drawing and books to plan his writing. I also discussed my role in helping him orchestrate a range of mechanics elements and integrate these mechanics with his content. In effect, I slipped in composing and revision within the "stage" of planning with and for him. I followed his lead, though, after I saw his interest in a particular topic or book. Rickey had his own personal style and way of integrating content and mechanics, and it was my role first to see it, then to understand it, and finally to devise ways to support and guide him. In his planning/composing/revising, Rickey worked *within* and *across* his pieces of writing, sharpening content and mechanics integration by moving forward to each new piece, and also backward to previous pieces. This self-initiated (and teacher-supported) process gave Rickey an increasingly deeper sense of his own direction and style as he moved toward "full-fledged authorship" (Moffett, 1988) for a kindergartner.

Revision and editing also speak to the delicate relationship between young writers and their sense of a writing voice and identity. The picture book author and illustrator Grace Lin ("The Extra Adjective," n.d.) reminds us that we often write and revise to become more like ourselves (or who we want to be) rather than writing to follow a particular genre.

> When I published my first book, *The Ugly Vegetables* (a story about my mother and I and the Chinese vegetables we grew when I was a child) I was thinking more about my personal story than a genre. So it was a little surprising to hear a fellow striving author/illustrator say to me, "It's good that you're using your culture—multicultural books are hot now. That's what's getting you published." Was it? Suddenly, the validation that I had broken through the publishing wall was marred by the idea that I had somehow squeezed through a back window. Was I only getting published because of my heritage and subject matter? Was I cheating? Was I selling out my culture for a career? (online)

Social Relationships

For Anne Haas Dyson (2000), children write and want to revisit the accuracy and content of their writing because their writing is part of the social and cultural fabric of the classroom. Children's peer culture and the "unofficial" ideas, experiences, ideas, and objects motivate young writers to write with verve, power, and with social cohesion and identity. In this view, the "peer relationships themselves—linked to the values and concerns of unofficial worlds—began to be mediated through writing" (Dyson, 2000, p. 56). What does this mean for editing and revising of content and mechanics? When we acknowledge the role of children's unofficial worlds in their writing, we can see that young writers revise and edit to deepen their connections with others and to insert themselves more strongly in the social and intellectual community of the classroom. As children talk and interact and revise alongside each other, they can draw on an expanded pool of possible "textual structures" (p. 57) to bring into their revision on their own or with the assistance of friends and peers.

New Language Learners

New language learners benefit from matching their linguistic knowledge and proficiencies with the demands of editing and revising. They must learn to decode, understand, and use the particular academic and school-based language of revision (*edit, editor, peer editing, symbol, insert, caret, unclear, voice,* and *audience*). Learning to improve the accuracy and voice of one's writing in a new language is a particularly challenging process. The children's book author Alma Flor Ada (n.d.) writes and revises with an awareness of her particular language fluencies and strengths.

> But in English, I found that I needed to depend more on the story—on the power of the story, because I can't do the playful things that I do with the language in Spanish, the puns, the rhymes, the alliterations—those things. I don't have that skill in English, so I need to depend on strong characters, strong plot, a good narrative, a good pace to get the kids interested. So, then I become a different person and a different writer in the other language, and that's, you know, part of the richness of being bicultural. (online)

Language Forms

When we ask young writers to revise and edit, which aspects of content and mechanics are we asking them (directly and covertly) to focus on? Which forms do we privilege ourselves? What surface features of written language do we want young writers to attend to most?

According to Lisa Delpit (1986, 1988, 1998, 2002), children need to carry their personal, communal, and culturally influenced experiences and ways of using oral and written language into the classroom for school success. Children need continual access and contact with each other to nurture these language ways in the classroom and in writing. Young writers benefit from access to these familiar forms *and* they also need expert guidance from us to understand and learn to use school-based forms. They need to acquire and internalize a range of possible "codes" for oral and written language to have at their disposal when they revise and edit. This helps young writers, especially some African-American students and other children of color, to learn to see how "different language forms are appropriate in different contexts" (1998, p. 53) and to add "another language form to the repertoire of African American children" (Delpit, 2002).

> We must make them feel welcomed and invited by allowing their interests, culture, and history into the classroom. We must reconnect them to their own brilliance and gain their trust so that they will learn from us. We must respect them, so that they feel connected to us. Then, and only then, might they be willing to adopt our language form as one to be added to their own. (p. 48)

The editing and revision process in writing must nurture young writers' familiar and trusted ways of using language, and also extend and move young writers toward new forms of content and mechanics integration.

STRATEGIES FOR EDITING AND REVISION

There are a number of basic strategies to integrate content and mechanics in the revision of young writers. In this section, I highlight the role of motivation, accuracy, selection, and conversation.

Motivation

Liz Goss, who teaches 2nd grade, defines *revision* as making changes to the "craft" and "content" of her students' writing. She defines *editing* as making changes to the "mechanics" such as spelling, punctuation, syntax, and mechanics particular to a certain genre. Liz wants her students to become "Writers with a capital W—people who have to write because that is what they do, like breathe or skip." Revision and editing are important components of Liz's strategies to guide her students to become "Writers."

> I have found that making writing authentic makes it much easier to motivate my students to revise and edit their work, which is where the main push for mechanics comes in. For example, if they know they are going to share their how-to books with the kindergartners, they will be more invested in correcting their writing and making a final copy with correct end marks, legible handwriting, etc. If they know their writing will become published in the school newspaper, they have more energy to proofread and really use their editing checklist. Before we have

a poetry café, they will be sure their piece has punctuation in ways a poet would use. They share works in progress as well, which helps them realize they forgot some mechanics.

Liz links revision and editing with the initial "goal" of writing for her students—to have a sense of purpose, to write for somebody, and to touch on some larger social and intellectual event or context. Reading with kindergartners, the school newspaper, and the poetry café are all examples of real audiences and venues for Liz's students to share their writing and get feedback. Their final written product does not signal the end of their composing and revising efforts; rather, the opportunities to share, perform, and discuss their writing with others essentially extend the composing and revision process. It is another chance, with varied audiences in varied venues, to revisit their writing.

James Britton (1987) believed that "education is *an effect of community*" [original emphasis] (p. 25). Liz's extension of editing and revision is "an effect" of the classroom community, school community, and outside communities. Writing for varied communities and for varied purposes pulls along Liz's students in their editing and revision, and also the other way around. It's a subtle distinction, but one that puts a primacy on contextualizing editing and revising within the larger goal of writing for a purpose and for others.

Liz has learned that editing and revision are challenging for her 2nd-graders.

> Young children do not always have a lot of desire to go back to a piece of writing to really edit or revise. I find they know how to use end marks, for example, but in their excitement about their content, their ideas, they often make simple mistakes with punctuation and other mechanics. I am not sure if a child of any age ever really wants to go back to a piece of writing, so I am not sure how much is developmental and how much is a natural feeling of wanting to be "done." But over time, they establish a habit of using certain mechanics *all* the time and build the endurance to revisit work and make it "stronger," i.e., to edit and revise. This is powerful learning for them: knowing they are doing the real work of writers as the craft and the mechanics become more integrated.

Liz emphasizes "a habit of using certain mechanics all the time," which instills a sense of confidence and competency in her students that they know what to edit, how, and why (at the 2nd-grade level). She also sees the value of building "endurance to revisit work and make it stronger," recognizing that effective revising and editing for her age group is largely dependent on emotional and physical "endurance" and stamina to go back over their writing.

Accuracy

Liz supports and guides her students' accuracy in revision and editing in three main ways:

1. attention to mechanics in isolation
2. focus on language variety and development
3. peer editing and checklists

Attention to Mechanics. Liz takes certain mechanics out of her writing curriculum and places them in separate mechanics lessons.

> While I use authentic writing and publishing often to show the importance of mechanics, I also periodically do a Daily Oral Language (DOL) activity where my students begin writing time by correcting sentences that I have created. It helps when I make the sentences about them, such as "terriel loves to read bok by Arnold lobel", and allow students to discuss how they corrected "my mistakes." This helps me isolate certain mechanics, such as noun-verb agreement or underlining book titles, and helps them practice finding and fixing mistakes separate from their own writing.

Liz's "periodic" instruction on mechanics in isolation as balanced with ongoing "authentic" writing echoes Lisa Delpit's (1988) advocacy of Courtney Cazden's (1988) dual approach toward content and mechanics.

1. Continuous opportunities for writers to participate in some authentic bit of the unending conversation . . . thereby becoming part of a vital community of talkers and writers in a particular domain, and
2. Periodic, temporary focus on conventions of form, taught as cultural conventions expected in a particular community. (p. 295)

Liz's isolated mechanics lessons are examples of a "periodic, temporary focus on conventions of form."

Language Variety and Development. Liz's students sometimes revise and edit on the computer, which helps them look at small chunks of language.

> I have found that having students type short pieces using Microsoft Word helps them see other ways of editing. They *love* to visually see the red line that indicates a misspelled world and they like to use the dictionary. They also begin to understand that the green line indicates a possible issue with grammar. It is still difficult for 8-year-olds to always choose the right word from the dictionary, but the computer is often a more interactive way for them to edit their work.

Computers motivate her students to revise and edit, and to talk with each other and Liz about misspelled words and the word-processing program's suggestions for changes in grammar. For instance, as Liz notes, most spell-checks will flag *ain't* and suggest *isn't* instead. For students who might put *ain't* in their dialogue in a story, this is an opportunity for Liz and the young writer to compare and contrast varied syntactical structures for the same word or phrase, and their effect on the content and style of the piece. By talking with her students about language usage and word choice arising from the flagging of a possible grammar "error," Liz avoids Michael Stubb's (2002) observation that "many teachers maintain the fiction that there is only one 'best' English for all purposes, and that this is the only proper English in the classroom" (p. 75).

Liz tells her students, all of whom are African American, that when they revise "there are multiple ways to say everything," and Liz balances students' familiar ways of speaking and writing with school-based forms.

> In terms of mechanics and content, I teach the students how to code-switch. I explain that the way they talk at home has a certain rhythm and a certain way of putting words together, and then there's what we call "school language" that many but not all books and genres are written in. We talk about how it sounds a little bit different, and I don't hint or say that standard English is the "right" one. There are multiple ways to say everything. So, especially with such mechanics as subject-verb agreement, adding "g's" onto the end of words, extra "be's" with verbs, we talk about the different ways to get across their ideas and different standards of how languages get put together in different contexts and for different purposes. I try to be explicit about it as much as it seems appropriate. There are other times when we get to play with it a bit more. For instance, in poetry there's a bit more freedom to decide which kind of languages to use and how they want to be expressive. Sometimes, we'll do parallel writing, when they write in their home voices and then they try it in their school voices. We do this so my students can name the languages they know and to help

them navigate school expectations for writing with certain kinds of mechanics. I try to balance the correctness of school with the richness of their home languages.

Liz uses editing and revising to link the surface elements of her students' written mechanics with an evolving integration of home and school language expectations, forms, and functions. As a teacher of Anglo-European origin, it's a process that demands knowledge of the linguistic and educational history of African-American children, and the need for multiple pathways toward acquiring additional oral and written language codes (Delpit, 1986, 1988, 1998, 2002).

Peer Editing and Checklists. Liz asks her students to revise and edit only certain written pieces and genres. For example, Liz uses a brief checklist for students to revise their how-to writing:

1. My steps make sense. I didn't forget a step.
2. I have a hook that grabs the reader.
3. I have a closing sentence that wraps up my story.
4. I used transition words.
5. My illustrations are clear.

Liz has her students publish their writing five to six times per year. For publishing, they handwrite all of their writing except their poetry, which they type on the computer since the poetry is shorter and doesn't take much time. For final publication, Liz has her students revise each other's work with a green pencil and refer to a revising sheet, and also edit each other's work with a red pen.

> When we get to the publishing stage, I have my students peer revise and peer edit. I have checklists for each child that include space for them to name their partner, so both are held accountable. It is important for them to know the expectations for content and mechanics—for example, an opening sentence that hooks the reader or all proper nouns capitalized. I also have them edit in red pen and revise in green pencil. This helps them see the changes more easily, but even more importantly it allows some excitement. It is fun to see how exciting a simple red pen is! Sometimes it doesn't take much!

Liz changes her checklists to match particular genres and forms of writing, such as this list for story writing:

1. __ I used sight and sound words.
2. __ My story has a beginning, middle, and end.
3. __ I added dialogue. (My mom said, "Wow!")
4. __ I used transition words. (Then, next)
5. __ I circled words I am not sure I spelled correctly.
6. __ I reread my work to be sure it makes sense.
7. __ My revising partner is _____.

Liz also uses an editing checklist of general mechanics elements pertinent to 2nd grade:

1. __ I did not use random capital letters.
2. __ I used end marks at the end of my writing. (. ? !)
3. __ My sentences start with a capital letter.
4. __ I capitalized people's names, months, and the word *I*.
5. __ I spelled word wall words correctly.
6. __ I tried to fix spelling mistakes.
7. __ I reread my work to be sure it makes sense.
8. __ My editing partner is _____.

The final publishing checklist is for individual children to check and reflect on their writing:

1. __ I used neat handwriting.
2. __ I included all of my revisions and corrections.
3. __ I used details in my pictures.
4. __ I wrote the title and author on the front cover.
5. __ I wrote a dedication.
6. __ I reread my work to be sure it is all correct.
7. __ What I am most proud of in my work:_____.
8. __ How I became a better writer:_____.

The publishing checklist focuses on mechanics, form, and content, and encourages students to revisit earlier edits and revisions. The list also encourages students to reflect in a general way on what they are most "proud of" in their writing, and how it has helped them become "a better writer."

Liz continually reflects on the value of these checklists, refining them as she learns more about her students' needs, capabilities, and talents. She also links editing and revising to assessment, and has developed a deeper understanding of where her students need to be in their writing development.

It is hard to find exemplars of 2nd-grade writing. I teach in a high-poverty school and it took me years to understand what reading on grade level looked like. In my classroom, only about four of my students come to me reading on grade level; the rest are below and a third are significantly below. This realization changed my urgency in how I taught reading. It made me raise the bar significantly for my students. I still struggle with making sure my expectations are high enough for my students in writing. It is difficult to know what is 2nd-grade writing. The state standards give a clue; examples of writing from books give a clue. The best source I have found is a very detailed three-part rubric from Linda Dorn and Carla Soffos's (2001) *Scaffolding Young Writers*. When I first used that rubric, I realized it held a very high standard for end-of-2nd-grade writing. From that rubric, I went backward through my year to map out quarter benchmarks for my students' development in writing content and mechanics.

Our Role as Editors

In our roles as editors in chief, it's a challenge to decide how much and how to help young writers edit and revise. Ilsa Miller, the 1st-grade teacher, sees her role as editor largely as observing, recording, and remembering each child's writing interests and needs. She is careful to focus on only one or two aspects of her young authors' writing when she helps them edit and revise.

> I looked at Jake's story [see Chapter 3] and realized that I really needed to do more with my students' story endings, but I eventually decided that it's best left for the 2nd-grade teacher. We then worked on peer editing and Ursula edited Jake's story. I have them peer edit because it seems like when they're editing someone else's paper they really see more than they do in their own paper. So Jake went back and revised and edited his story. I also took time to edit and revise my story about when my son got hurt at Costco, which I had modeled for the class during our planning phase. I often tell them that I'm going to edit one thing. I might say, "Today we're just looking for capitals, or we're just looking for periods," because I find at this age that if you don't separate out certain elements of content and mechanics, it's just too much for a lot of them.

Ilsa continues her modeling of effective content and mechanics integration in her editing and revising, which continues a developmental and teaching link from planning to composing to editing and revising.

> As teachers, we need to be models of revisers for our students, showing them how to learn and improve, showing them that revising isn't just for kids who don't know as much as we do about writing and reading. (Bissex, 1996, p. 151)

Showing young writers how and why we revise and edit our writing not only serves as a model of revision, but also shows students that we are also "learning and improving."

> If they see us write, they will see the middle process, the hidden ground—from the choice of topic to the completion of the work. Teachers don't have to be expert writers to "write" with the children. In fact, there may be an advantage in growing with them, learning together as both seek to find meaning in writing. (Graves, 1983, p. 42)

By the "middle process" and "hidden ground," Graves is referring to all the planning, composing, and editing and revising that happens between a young writer's initial inspiration for writing and the final written product. Revision and editing are an integral part of this middle ground.

Ilsa's revising and editing of her own writing lengthens the learning process about content and mechanics for her students, and extends the teaching time that Ilsa devotes to identifying and teaching key connections between content and mechanics. This process helps Ilsa pinpoint the particular editing and revision talents and needs of each individual student.

> Elsa is a very confident writer who wrote a story about her family: "My family was eating dinner in the dining room. Me and my mom and dad and crazy brother were talking happily. Chatter. Chatter. Chatter. Bang! All of a sudden the lights went out. Me and my mommy screamed a small scream 'aaaah' and then we got our wits back. We walked to the pantry. It was difficult to walk because we kept bumping into walls and each other. When we finally reached the pantry we got the flashlight and some candles. I was really excited. I loved being in the dark. Then we turned off the lights and I went to bed. The next day the lights were back on."
>
> Elsa is someone who's really working on word choice. She's very aware of it. And then there is Cedi, who was really into writing about small moments and just zooming in, and he wanted to write about the feelings that he had the first time he went on a plane right before it went up into the air: "I was getting on a plane and I felt scared and excited at the same time. As I got on the plane it was the first time I had been on a plane. I was going down a long tube and I start going into the plane. As I walked down the aisles I saw the conductor. I sat down and buckled my seat belt. Then I started going up and up."

> Cedi really wanted to write more, but he was having a hard time knowing which details to write about and what to abandon and so he just ended it.

Given her awareness of Elsa's interest in word choice and Cedi's interest in small moments, Ilsa could focus on these particular aspects of their writing as she helped them revise and edit. Her knowledge of her students' interests and needs *at the moment* of editing and revision, allows Ilsa to make quick and informed choices about how much and what to help her students edit and revise.

Joli Gordon, in 3rd grade, also carefully considers her role as editor and the extent to which she helps her students edit their writing.

> We heavily rely on mentor texts for revision and editing ideas. I also refrain from sitting with a child, and since most of us want to change mechanics like grammar and punctuation, saying things like, "You know, you really need to put these two sentences together." I refrain from heavy editing. If I don't, then it becomes my writing and not their writing. I'd rather have them help each other than have me do it. I want them to take more ownership. And a lot of times I partner them with another child and I say, "You know what? You want help with more so-phisticated words or you want bigger words? Go work with Toby; he's our wordsmith. Oh, you need help with details? Go work with Lucy, she's great with details."

For Joli to pair students together for peer revision, Joli has to know her students well both as writers and as individuals.

> I know my students as writers because I see them every day. We write every day. I only have 20 children so I'm often more of a delegator dur-ing revision and editing. They sometimes explain it to each other better than I can. I put a lot on them in 3rd grade—it's not just coming from me. I'm like the last step of the process. I meet and conference with them, and often I'll say, "What do you need? Okay, well, how do you think you can go about that?" I try to elicit their own ideas for improvement. I also want them to hear editing and revision ideas from their friends. Nine times out of ten, their friends would say the same thing I would say. I just add in a few things. Our writing, and our editing and revision time, is very social. Writing is very social. It's not loud but it's not quiet in here. There's definitely a buzz during writing. They love writing. They really, re-ally get into it. They're working together. They're sharing. They're talking. They're making decisions.

Joli carefully observes and tracks her students' editing and revising needs, and links the particular need of a student at a particular moment with another young writer in the class. In this way, Joli uses editing and revision to promote a community of writers who are also editors and revisers for each other.

Sarah Carp, teaching 4th grade, sees her role as editor as selecting particular content and mechanics in her students' writing to attune their revising skills. She is particularly interested in helping her new language learners learn the nuanced and subtle aspects of sound, form, and function in a new language.

> Editing and revising are related to my students hearing, self-correcting, being able to hear what their language sounds like, and knowing if they like the way it sounds. When I'm writing, I ask myself, "Does it sound like I've said enough?" "Do I want to add something?" It's not an objective thing. It's about training our ears. One of the challenges of finding that balance is deciding how much to correct in a student's writing and letting go of my own hopes or dreams that they'll come up with perfect papers to show their parents. I think parents have that expectation, too, or have a desire that it would be nice to see a perfect paper from their child. I think a lot of times those perfect papers are filled with corrections from me that the students actually don't understand or aren't internalizing. They're just copying or saying they understand my edits. I'm now trying to focus the corrections and editing, linking them to certain skills, so that my students can improve themselves as writers with these skills. It's a constant challenge. For example, the book review that we're doing now is a five-paragraph essay, but I decided to really just edit the first two paragraphs with my students.

Like Joli, Sarah asks questions such as "Does it sound like you've said enough?" that help children learn their own strategies for focusing on content and mechanics in revision and editing. As Lucy Calkins (2006) notes, "The most sophisticated and important sort of revision" is "exploratory" as writers "venture into unexplored terrain and stumble upon new insights that illuminate a topic not only for the reader but also for the writer" (p. 17).

Teaching new language learners, Sarah helps them attune their ear to the sounds of words, formats, and structures in a new language. Sarah also continually monitors the appropriateness of her editing and revision goals and expectations.

> I notice that when I look at the five paragraphs and I see a lot of mistakes, I wish that they would write less or if I were editing all five

paragraphs myself, I would start to take shortcuts and short-circuit the whole editing and revision process. So I am now letting my students write these long pieces, and then I correct only the first half with them and the second half they do on their own or with a peer to internalize some of the editing. This is the first time that I've tried this approach. When I started to correct their mechanics in their 3- to 4-page papers, it became too overwhelming. There were too many facets to it, too many things that I would need to teach each student for them to understand how and why I am editing and revising their piece with them. I'm also figuring out how much I want to correct and perfect their writing before it makes sense to move on to something else and keep the ideas flowing and keep the pen flowing. I don't want to disrupt the rhythm or the flow of the writing in the class by spending a week and a half editing something. I'm trying instead to spend a lot more time planning. I used to only spend a class period brainstorming and a class period planning, and now I'm increasing our time on planning their writing around a topic. I now spend a lot more time planning than I was originally giving my students because I wanted to jump into the revising and editing.

By looking closely at what her students are actually writing, and reflecting her effectiveness as an editor, Sarah has pared down and tightened her editing and revision goals. Lucy Calkins (1986) underscores Sarah's efforts to streamline her editing and revising.

> When we, as teachers, pull our chairs alongside young writers and try to understand their ways of understanding, when we search for the logic in their errors and the patterns in their growth, then we no longer spin our wheels. (p. 32)

Sarah now experiments with a new approach that provides a model for making corrections in terms of content and especially mechanics, and then has her young writers continue to edit on their own or with peers. This two-step revision process of teacher modeling and self/peer revision is an example of a "gradual release of responsibility" from teacher to student (Miller, 2002) to promote greater internalization of content and mechanics integration.

Sarah has also simplified and strengthened her editing and revision process for herself and her students by devoting more time to planning and composing. She has spread out editing and revising across what Donald Graves (1983) called the mysterious "middle ground" between a writer's initial inspiration and the final written product. Graves (1994) also points out that young writers need not always revise a current piece because they often "display new skills in the next piece they write." This idea helps us see how we can stretch out editing and revising *across* the pieces that children write, and we are not always bound and confined to editing everything within a single piece before moving on.

Conversation

When we can "pull our chairs alongside young writers" (Calkins, 1986, p. 32), we can talk individually with young writers about their editing and revision. It allows us to tailor our language—what we say and how we say it—to individual young writers, and to develop a relationship with each child as a writer.

Kindergarten: Vanessa. I worked with Vanessa, a Spanish speaker learning English in kindergarten, for several months in a small-group format. In early November, Vanessa wrote about and drew different topics in her journal (Figure 5.1).

Vanessa had been exploring the blank pages in her journal by drawing and writing with me and the other children in our small group. By November, Vanessa had learned that she could draw and write about more than one topic per journal entry, and that talking with her peers and with me as she wrote and drew spurred on her ideas. She carried out six different but interrelated composing processes (reading a text, copying a text, copying a picture, drawing on her own, dictating to me, and writing on her own) that resulted in six different products:

1. from looking at *Chicka Chicka Boom Boom* (Archambault & Martin, 1989), she wrote the alphabet from A to Z, complete with both upper- and lowercase letters
2. dictating to me, "I just wrote Chicka Chicka. It's the greatest story in the world"
3. drawing a coconut tree with a coconut
4. writing "chicka chicka boom boom"
5. switching topics and drawing a dolphin, flowers, a butterfly, clouds, and a sun
6. with my assistance, she wrote, "The Dlfn was HvnG Fun."

Her conversations with her peers provided also Vanessa, a new language learner, with oral language practice in English and the opportunity to maintain her Spanish. The opportunity to speak in both Spanish and English with her friends provided a form of editing and revision as she drew and wrote. They exchanged ideas about what to draw and write, and they

Figure 5.1. Vanessa's November Drawing and Writing

even gave each other suggestions and strategies for how to write in the blank space on the page, the selection of colors of markers, style of writing, word choice, and spellings. In this way, the opportunities for dual-language conversation enriched Vanessa's editing and revising and pulled it back into her planning and composing phases—all three phases were squashed into one.

By June, Vanessa had simplified the total number of composing processes and also her written products (Figure 5.2). She had moved on from experimenting and playing with multiple composing processes and products in one journal entry, and had settled into a routine of focusing on a drawing and a written text. By June, Vanessa had also learned to see me as a conversational partner for editing and revising content and mechanics, and I in turn had learned more about her linguistic, literacy, and developmental capabilities.

Vanessa and her friend Kristina, with whom she spoke in Spanish and English, both liked to draw and write about suns, stars, flowers, and animals. The girls usually drew first, looking at one another's drawings and talking as they went. Vanessa had started the habit of marking off a space for her future writing with straight and wavy lines (Figure 5.2). This became

Figure 5.2. Vanessa's Dancing Stars

an editing strategy, as she figured out ahead of time how much room she wanted to devote to her text and how much she wanted to devote to her drawing. By June, she usually settled for a 50–50 ratio of text to drawing.

Vanessa told me that she wanted "The stars are dancing" for her first sentence. She knew from memory how to spell most of *the* and wrote "t-h-g," and then erased the "g" and wrote in "e" when I asked her if the last letter was an "e." For *star*, I asked Vanessa what it started with and she wrote "s." I then made the sound /t/ for "t" and she wrote "t." I said, "The end of *star* is hard. The next letter is 'a' (which she wrote) and then the last letter is for the /r/ sound (and she wrote "r")." For *are*, I told Vanessa the entire spelling, which she wrote down. For *dancing*, she wrote "d" on her own and I said a short /a/ sound and she wrote "a." I made the /n/ sound for "n," but she wrote an "r." I slowly said "dancing" and emphasized the /s/ for "c," and Vanessa watched me say the word and then wrote an "s" for the "c." I said "ing" and Vanessa wrote "ing" since she had memorized this suffix from her classroom.

She wanted to write, "The moon is shining" for her next sentence, nicely paralleling the syntactical structure of the first sentence. Vanessa wrote *the* and then an "M" for moon. She then looked puzzled. "/oo/ is hard," I said. "It has two of the same letters, "o" and an "o" for /oo/." Vanessa wrote "oo." "Then the last letter is . . . say 'moon' again and what do you hear at the end?" She did not say anything. "It's in your name." And I said it slowly and drew it out and slightly accented the "n" in her name. "N," she said and wrote it down. She then repeated the whole sentence out loud as if to remember what to write next, and wrote *is* on her own as a known sight word from her classroom. For *shining*, Vanessa wrote "s" and then I decided to skip the "h" entirely and go to the "n," and I said the sound /n/ and Vanessa wrote an "n." "And now—"ing," and you are done," I said, and Vanessa added it to "san" to make "saning."

Opportunities for this kind of one-on-one conversation help ensure developmentally appropriate revision and editing support for children's particular needs.

3rd Grade: Madhuvanti and Ayumi.
Madhuvanti, who teaches 3rd grade, emphasizes conversation during one-on-one writing conferences with each student as he or she composes. By spending a good deal of time with students *as they compose*, Madhuvanti brings in editing and revising before they finish their writing.

> Revision makes more sense, really true revision, makes more sense while students are in draft form if you're able to check in with them fairly frequently. The problem with revision comes when students have

written five pages of handwritten work and you come back in and you
say, "Oh, here in paragraph two," it's heartbreaking for them. I think
revision might be overrated unless you can really talk to the children
at least once a week, as they're in progress, and give them points to
revise while they're in that moment. Writing partners and frequent
conferences give the opportunity for that. A structured writer's workshop approach let's you think about revision, and encourages students
to think about revision as more of an active writing phase rather than,
"Here's the five pages that I've written and now I'm going to go back
and change something that's easy to change."

Madhuvanti's philosophy of front-loading revision and editing has several
key instructional benefits:

1. It saves students time and energy later on, as they've already done
   some revision and editing.
2. It improves their later editing and revision because they've already thought about what they might change from talking with
   Madhuvanti.
3. The one-on-one conversations help students revise and edit out
   loud, allowing their oral language talents to strengthen their
   writing.
4. The conversations give students new ideas for editing and revision
   that they bring back to their writing partners.
5. Students also do the opposite, bringing editing and revising ideas
   from their writing partner to their conversations with Madhuvanti.
6. Madhuvanti's frequent conversations with students as they compose keep her up to date with individual children's writing—their
   latest deletions, additions, story events, character development,
   information.

Madhuvanti talks with each child in her class over the course of
2 weeks. She also teaches her students certain editing marks, such as the
caret and asterisk for insertion or addition of extra material. Madhuvanti
has her students write on only one side of their writing journal pages and
use the blank page for adding in longer revisions "without having to do a lot
of rewriting." Her students use only a pencil with no eraser for composing
and editing.

I have them use a pencil with no eraser so when they do make a
mistake or they're unhappy with something they can just scratch it out
with one line so we can both see all of their revision and editing. At this

grade level, there are also some students who perseverate and want perfection, so the lack of an eraser helps them get going and move ahead. For example, they'll write a sentence and decide, "Oh well, it's not quite what I wanted but. . . ." It helps them keep moving. I also want to see what changes they've made, and I want my students to see their revisions and edits so that they can celebrate if they chose a different word that fits better or crossed out a word that they saw, once they'd written it, was actually spelled incorrectly.

In late January, Madhuvanti worked with Ayumi on her "Stolen Necklace" story. Ayumi had already mapped out her basic story plot as a story arc or story mountain on a piece of paper. The arc contained 8 squares within which Ayumi wrote just enough text (see below) to create a trajectory of her story:

- Square 1. She [Victoria/Viki] is in her sister's [Rosalie] room about to steal something.
- Square 2. She steals her sister's favorite necklace that she wears everyday.
- Square 3. She keeps it in her box. But one day, her friend comes over.
- Square 4. She wants to see inside the box.
- Square 5. They forced her to open the box.
- Square 6. They found out that she gets in big trouble.
- Square 7. For her sister's birthday, Viki gives her a necklace.
- Square 8. Viki's sister forgives her.

Ayumi subsequently made certain revisions to her story arc. For example, she added "her sis starts looking for the necklace" and put in an arrow pointing to Square 3 in the story arc. For Square 4, Ayumi wrote "Viki's sis" and drew an arrow to insert this explanation in between the "She" and the "wants" in the sentence, "She wants to see inside her box." The revision of a graphic organizer or any planning visual, as Ayumi has done here, helps young writers resee and rethink the content of their writing as they compose and edit.

Ayumi had written four pages of her story when she sat down with Madhuvanti to discuss possible changes.

>   *Madhuvanti:* Let's see where you are now. (Ayumi starts to give an overview of where she is in her story at the moment.) And then what? (Ayumi reads a bit of her text.) So who runs off with the necklace?

Ayumi: Victoria. [Victoria has taken her sister Rosalie's bracelet]

Madhuvanti: (reading the section of Ayumi's story out loud) It seems a little sudden and strange that Victoria just runs off after Rosalie takes the bracelet back. What would *your* sister do?

Ayumi: She'd say, "What's wrong with you?!"

Madhuvanti: OK. (reads more text out loud) "Had taken" (writes in "taken" for Ayumi's "took"). "Had ignored me" (writes in "had" with a caret between Ayumi's "she" and "ignored"). (continuing to read out loud) That's a nice touch (commenting that the character Victoria knew her father's telephone number). Who is saying, "Fine, I'll pay for it?"

Ayumi: My dad.

Madhuvanti: For the birthday present?

Ayumi: Yes.

Madhuvanti: A whole lot of time passes here, and so have people forgiven each other?

Ayumi: They didn't talk to each other.

Madhuvanti: You might want to clue the reader in since it's been a few weeks. (Madhuvanti reads more out loud) Tell me what this sentence means.

Ayumi: Wishing it was a sad trip. (Madhuvanti writes "clarify" in the left margin for Ayumi's later revision, and later Ayumi changes the sentence to a "horrible dream")

Madhuvanti: (continuing to read out loud) I *had* to open it. It's past tense, not present tense. (Ayumi's text is "I have to open it" and Madhuvanti writes "had" above the "have"). Ah, a nice twist. (i.e., Rosalie giving Victoria the necklace that she had initially stolen from her) Now how is it going to end?

Ayumi: Am not sure.

Madhuvanti: If you were *really* in this story, what would you do? Would there be a conversation between the two sisters? What would you say?

Ayumi: I don't know yet.

Madhuvanti: You've got some thinking to do.

Madhuvanti uses the conference to talk with Ayumi about ways to strengthen content and mechanics integration. She does not directly talk about this integration with Ayumi, but does directly edit a few mechanics and note possible content changes. Madhuvanti also leaves some revising ideas for Ayumi to decide on later on. Ayumi's final draft (Figure 5.3) incorporates Madhuvanti's direct changes as well as Ayumi's own edits based on Madhuvanti's suggestions and questions.

Figure 5.3. Ayumi's Final Draft of "The Stolen Necklace"

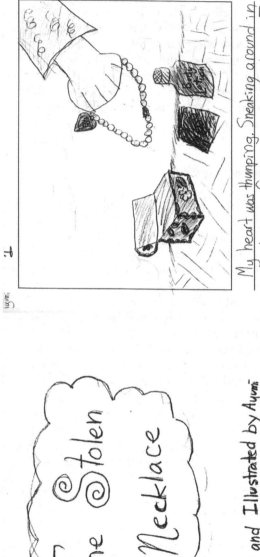

The Stolen Necklace

Written and Illustrated by Ayumi

My heart was thumping. Sneaking around in your sisters room for revenge was not easy. I was afraid that I might be caught. My mom called me. "Victoria! Dinner!" I grabbed my sister's necklace and hid it in my box. At least I was safe. Dinner didn't taste good as usual. I felt guilty but not enough to admit what I had done. At night I tossed and turned. I woke up sweating. The next morning, I had dark shadows under my eyes.

My sister Rosalie was down on her knees under her desk. I knew what she was looking for. Even though I knew, I asked, "What are you looking for?" She replied, "My necklace. Have you seen it?" Just then my mom said, "Victoria! Clean up your room! Your friend is coming!" My friend? My best friend Hannie was coming over? I hurried to clean up my room. It seemed like ages before Hannie came over

But when she came over, all she wanted to know was what was in my secret box. Then my sister joined in. Soon they were chanting, "Show us? Show us?" Finally, Rosalie lunged for it but my hand was quicker. I held it tight but it was no use. It was 2 against 1. Hannie loosened my fingers while Rosalie took the box. They opened the box together. I burst out of my room before I saw the look on their faces.

Ayumi 3

She left as quickly as possible. Now it was just me & Rosalie. I felt my face getting hot. After awhile, Rosalie busted into words. She said I was a trouble maker so I told her it was for revenge. Then Rosalie said I was a little creep. I couldn't bear it. I had told my mom 100 times that Rosalie had taken my best note book and didn't return it!!

Ayumi 4

Rosalie lunged after me with the necklace trailing from her hand. I felt like I was playing cat and mouse and I was the mouse. I ran from room to room finally ending up in my room where Rosalie caught me. I felt terrible. I wished I could turn into air and float away. "I think I have to go now" Hannie said.

Ayumi: 6

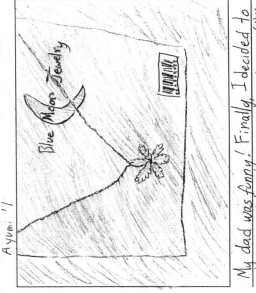

But she had ignored me every time. Then my sister rushed to mom and tattled about her necklace. Mom believed her right away and I didn't have allowance for a week. Luckily, Rosalie's birthday was near so I decided not to give her a birthday present. My dad was living far away so I called him for advice. I laughed and giggled over the phone.

Ayumi: 11

Blue Moon Jewelry

My dad was funny! Finally, I decided to ask him. I told him my story and he said, "Maybe, you should give her a necklace for her birthday." "No way!" I almost yelled into the phone. We argued and argued until my dad said, "Fine! I'll pay for it but you have to choose." Then I gave in and he sent me the money privately. I went to the jewelry shop and brought a pretty snowflake necklace. For Rosalie's birthday, I gave her a glare.

Happy Birthday Victoria

Rosalie's Present

The necklace was in my box. I was not going to give Rosalie the necklace. By December it was my birthday at last, not Rosalie's. My friends gave me some presents at school but I wasn't allowed to open them until I got home. Under all the presents, there was one that said, "To: Victoria From: Rosalie." I saved that one for last. When all the presents were unwrapped I realized I forgot Rosalie's.

It was wrapped in pink with little sparkles on it. I was wishing hard this was a horrible dream and I was going to wake up soon. I didn't want to open it. I had to open it. No I didn't. I wanted to get it over with it quickly. When I opened the present from Rosalie, there lay a necklace made of pearls. It was very familiar. It was the necklace I had stolen! "I thought you wanted it so I gave it to you." Rosalie said.

Ayum: 10

So, I said, "You keep it. I stole it from you."
"You keep it," Rosalie retorted. "Fine!" Then wait!"
I said and went to my room. I took out the
snowflake necklace from my box. Then, I wrapped
it up in Rosalie's favorite color. Purple. I rushed
back to Rosalie and handed the wrapped present
over. I took the pearl necklace from Rosalie and said,
"Thanks." Since then, everything's turned back to
normal and Rosalie and I have had only mildly serious
fights.

Madhuvanti directly changes elements of Ayumi's mechanics (changing verb tenses, adding words) and also elements of content (asking clarifying questions about plot, character, language). Madhuvanti mixes and matches the specificity and directness of her content and mechanics comments; having known Ayumi's writing since September, Madhuvanti knows how much to revise and edit right then and there with Ayumi, and how much she can ask Ayumi to figure out later on her own. Madhuvanti's strategy of reading Ayumi's story out loud also allows Ayumi to rehear and rethink certain elements of content and mechanics. It allows Madhuvanti and Ayumi to revisit the text together, and gives them a focal point for their conversation about revision and editing.

4th Grade: Sarah and Jorge. Sarah Carp balances the expectations of content and mechanics integration in 4th grade with the needs and talents of her new language learners. Sarah also carefully keeps in mind her students' feelings during revising and editing.

> We revisit the mechanics in the revision process and peer editing. First, though, they have to be invested in their ideas and excited about them; then they want to correct their writing and make their writing more comprehensible. In revision and editing, I really consider the students' feelings and how hurtful it can be sometimes to see that red pen from me all over the paper. I don't even think they learn from our correcting of every mistake. It's so jarring and just flattens their motivation. So I try to avoid the red pen and use another color. We also try to edit for one thing at a time.

Like Amanda and Madhuvanti, Sarah talks with her students *as* they plan and write, and works with her students on their editing and revising before they have "finished" a piece of writing.

> English language learners benefit from an adult sitting and talking with them while they're composing. For these students, they have an idea and then by the time it gets on the paper, then it's really confusing. It's sometimes easier to correct them when it's in the oral place; once it's written down, then there's something sensitive about saying, "Oh, let's erase this whole thing or scratch it out." These students also need help translating from one language to another—many of their translations don't sound quite right or make sense in English.

Sarah preempts editing and revision as an end-of-writing stage, and since thoughts and ideas rarely directly transfer from one language to another, Sarah helps her students with word choice and syntax in English.

For some students, a good conversation is enough and then they can just write on their own if they have an internalization of English syntax and organization. I also have a few students who need support with every sentence since their sentences in English are either very simple or have grammatical issues that make comprehension difficult for others. For these students, I talk through their ideas to increase their sense of ownership of their words. This process makes them feel relieved because they have ideas and can begin to say to themselves, "Oh, I get it now." With editing and revision, it's always a challenge to explain every edit to a student. And I don't really like doing edits that don't have any teachable moments. I help them edit their work so that next time or a few times later, students will notice the mistake themselves. So I want to explain everything, why we're doing it, why it sounds better, but then that takes a lot of time and it has to be one-on-one. I want them to eventually practice revision somewhat independently and with peers.

In January, Sarah had her class write a five-paragraph book review on their independent reading book. Jorge chose Roald Dahl's (1988) *Matilda*. Before they started to write, Sarah and the class read a few sample book reviews and also asked each student to take notes on their book, noting key events and other elements as "evidence from the text." To more easily see their format for revision purposes, Sarah asked her students to write each paragraph on a separate sheet of paper. Sarah talked with each student as they edited and revised their book review, and the students also did peer editing. Jorge's piece needed little editing, since "he tends to write with few errors."

With Sarah, with a classmate, and on his own, Jorge revised his spelling (*Imagen* to *Imagine*, *they're son* to *their son*), edited the syntax (the pronoun *their* as in "their parents" to "her parents"), added capital letters (*her* at the start of a sentence to *Her*, as indicated with the editing mark of three lines underneath his original "h"). Sarah helped with a few spelling words, writing in *extraordinary* for Jorge's *extradanary* and *probably* for Jorge's *probaly*.

According to Sarah, Jorge "is a native Spanish speaker and comes from a Spanish-only household. Toward the end of the year, he was redesignated as no longer an ELL because his English was so strong. He has an excellent vocabulary in both languages and incredible language skills." Sarah pointed out that Jorge's sentence in the second paragraph, "Matilda actually has the guts to put super glue in her dad's rakish looking hat," was of his own invention as he "emulated Roald Dahl's voice and style." After she read this line, Sarah "shared Jorge's adoption of Dahl's style with the class and we talked about the interesting words that Dahl uses like *rakish*." Dahl's actual sentence from *Matilda* is "He thought it gave him a rakish daring look, especially when he wore it at an angle with his loud checked jacket and green tie" (p. 30).

There are additional elements of content and mechanics that Sarah decided not to ask Jorge to edit and revise. These include nuances of English phrasing (e.g., Jorge's "Her life has a grand level of difficulty" and "This book is for people of all ages and that like funny books"); clarity in meaning ("Her life is probably about 75% books); forming compound words ("your self"); and fixing lowercase versus uppercase ("the mean headmistress treats all kids like punching bags"). Sarah wants to avoid over-editing, and does not want Jorge and other students to become so bogged down in editing that they lose the interest and motivation to write their final published piece and move on to the next.

As Madhuvanti did with Ayumi, Sarah knows that Jorge will make additional edits and revisions on his own when he works on his final published piece. In his final draft, Jorge made a word choice revision ("Matilda is very *rakish*" became "Matilda is very *smart*"); a change in spelling ("woulden't" corrected to "wouldn't"); and a subtle change in word meaning ("Would your parents *care if* you go to the library by your self?" was revised to "Would your parents *let you* go to the library by your self?").

Matilda, A Book Review, By Jorge

Imagine an astounding kid being treated like a twit by her parents. Matilda's life is not an average kid's life. Her life has a grand level of difficulty. She is smart but her parents hate her. Roald Dahl wrote many books like *Matilda*. The style is very unique and the events are very exaggerated.

Furthermore, Matilda's life is extraordinary. To her parents Matilda is a prankster. Matilda actually has the guts to put super glue in her dad's rakish looking hat. Matilda is very smart. 2 × 478 is not even close to hard for Matilda. She is the most gifted person I know. Her life is probably about 75% books.

In addition, her parents are the worst you can have. Matilda's parents are so dim-witted. By that I mean who wouldn't notice super glue in their hat. They also don't care about Matilda. Would your parents let you go to the library by your self? In other words they only care about their son.

However, her life is no different at school. The mean head mistress treats all kids like punching bags. That is nothing like her nice teacher Miss Honey. Matilda's life is mostly ruined because she is the main target for the head mistress.

Do you think you can outsmart Matilda? I would recommend this book for people of all ages and that like funny books.

———————————

Revision and editing are challenging for young writers and for us as teachers of writing. Revision and editing challenge us to look at the particulars of content and mechanics, and to see how and where we can make our mechanics more accurate and our content more engaging and comprehensible. It is critical that we make a place for revision and editing early on in children's writing—when they plan and compose—and not save it all for later. Effective revision and editing are affected by several key factors, including the internal/external dimensions of texts and speech, premeditation and reflection, social relationships, and particular support for new language learners. Revision and editing can be strengthened by increasing young writers' motivation and accuracy, our careful selection of what to edit and when in students' writing, and opportunities for us to talk one-on-one with students about where and how to integrate content and mechanics.

Chapter 6

A WRITING MIND

Writing well for young writers is an involved and long-term process. It demands a high level of concentration, physical effort, confidence, risk-taking, perseverance, knowledge, and accuracy. Although we have ample theory and research on teaching writing to young writers over the last 40 years, we continue to need new ways to deepen our teaching knowledge of what it means to write well and ways to support and guide children's learning.

In this book, I have provided background history on significant research and practice on children's early literacy and writing development. I also presented the insights and teaching strategies of seven wonderful teachers of writing across the K–4 span. In addition, I included my own work with kindergarten-age children. This book has focused on the integration of content and mechanics in writing education, and the power of our teaching minds to deepen and strengthen our teaching of writing. I close the book with a brief discussion of three key ideas—accuracy and inventiveness with mechanics, originality and creativity, and the evolving teaching mind.

AN INVENTIVENESS WITH MECHANICS

The last 15 years have seen a proliferation of standards, testing, and published curriculum programs in writing policy and practice. The primary emphasis in this movement has been on written language mechanics. These mechanics and conventions are more easily seen by children and adults, more easily quantifiable, and more easily positioned within a scope and sequence of expectations and teaching than content and meaning in writing. An emphasis on written language mechanics and conventions, when properly done and kept in moderation, is crucial for all young writers, because mechanics form a critical foundation for learning to write well. They are as basic and intrinsic to writing well as balance and pedaling and steering are to riding a bicycle well. Yet, as I've discussed and the seven teachers have

134

shown in this book, rich and effective writing instruction is not envisioned and sustained on mechanics alone. Writing and learning to write well, even for young children, is more sophisticated and more high-level.

The primary grade years are the critical period for children's development and for our inculcating a *learning mind* for young writers. This learning mind is the parallel process and phenomenon to our teaching mind. It encompasses who children are as individuals and as members of learning communities in and out of school settings. It touches on how children see themselves as learners and as writers—actors in the evolving realm of words and ideas and images and sounds. Written language mechanics are an integral part of this growth and development. And, most critically, accuracy with and internalization of written language mechanics improves and deepens when integrated with written language content.

Mechanics need not appear alone at the starting line of the journey toward writing well; they can and must be joined with content and meaning. As we move forward, as shown by the teachers in this book, we can emphasize mechanics and content in planning, composing, editing, and revising. Writing well is almost always, ultimately, about putting together content and mechanics in ways that bear the personal imprint of young writers, say something of import to young writers and to others, and contain some mix of internal and external beauty and synchrony.

The happy confluence of mechanics and content often comes about through the breaking down of written language elements within the context of content-rich writing education. This is Lisa Delpit's (1986, 1988, 1998, 2002) "expert knowledge"—insider knowledge of how, where, when, and for whom language and literacy can become powerful ways for all children to write well. The breaking down of written language mechanics and affixing them to bits and pieces of content is a wonderfully (and at times frustrating) inventive and creative process. This process, if it can be called that, demands a high level of human attention, observation, concentration, synthesis, and shaping.

> Languages and music both demand the control of masses of detail, so organized that they can be sorted out with unconscious speed. Griscom's achievements in these fields undoubtedly conditioned his way of thinking and, in addition to his training as a first-rate biologist, helped make him the field man he was. The mind of a good field observer works like a kaleidoscope, the gadget of our childhood, wherein loose fragments of colored glass fall quickly into symmetrical patterns. We see a bird. With an instinctive movement we center it in our glass. All the thousands of fragments we know about birds—locality, season, habitat, voice, actions, field marks, and likelihood of occurrence—flash across the mirrors of the mind and fall into place—and we have the name of our bird. (Peterson, 2006, p. 220)

Although Roger Tory Peterson is describing the process of identifying a bird, his emphasis on observation, detail, accuracy, and the powers of the human mind are all pertinent to learning to write well. Writing is also an endeavor that involves "masses of detail" to be "organized" so that "they can be sorted out with unconscious speed." Written language mechanics and conventions, to the emerging writing minds of young writers, are part of the "masses of detail." Young writers are learning to approach writing as looking at a "kaleidoscope . . . wherein loose fragments of colored glass" (the elements of mechanics) "fall quickly into symmetrical patterns" when affixed to elements of content and meaning. As young writers grow and develop, and increase their inventiveness with mechanics, their knowledge and facility with a potentially infinite possible number of "fragments" increases and deepens. There is then an increased "likelihood of occurrence" of mechanics and content "falling into place," and then finally we have the "name" of the right structure, format, syntax, and spelling falling into place with the right idea, feeling, information, plot, and character. And when this happens over and over again for young writers, with our expert guidance, the "likelihood" of this confluence increases and becomes more second nature.

ORIGINALITY AND CREATIVITY

Accuracy and inventiveness with written language mechanics need their close cousins—originality and creativity in written language content and meaning. Originality and creativity bubble up in writing education when we remember Delpit's (2002) adage that we "must first make our students recognize their potential brilliance" (p. 46). Young writers thrive on writing education that is founded upon the "potential brilliance" of their linguistic, cultural, and personal talents and resources. Our integration of content and mechanics must speak carefully to children's sense of self as members of dynamic and ever-changing social and intellectual communities. Writing well, with its key foundation of content and mechanics integration, relies on enlisting children's interests and motivation and drive—their "ambition."

The intangibles of writing well challenge young writers to feel and believe that they have something to say and can say it well. Young writers in the K–4 span, especially younger students and those learning a new language, need our support to *believe* that they will write even when they *know* they can't write well at the moment. What often pulls young writers along toward the attainment of engaging content and accurate mechanics is a hoped-for future treasure. This treasure is the treat of a well-formed story, a never-before-created character, a funny scene, an informative piece, a set of inventive rhymes. The treasure for kindergarten-age Thyra is her space story (see the Introduction) and the wonderment of the ET moment of a "space ship landing in my backyard." The treasure for 2nd-grader Cristian is his how-to piece on baseball (also in the Introduction) and the chance to write about baseball with a succinctness ("Now you know how to play baseball") not even seen in the writing of the great baseball writer Roger Angell. The treasure is kindergarten-age Rickey's joy and delight in linking science, art, and writing in his squirrel story and drawing (Chapter 3). The treasure for Ayumi is the satisfaction of creating twists of plot as played out against sibling rivalry in "The Stolen Necklace" (Chapter 5). The treasure for Jorge is adopting the language and style of Roald Dahl in his book review of *Matilda* (Chapter 5).

The discovery of the treasures of writing well is the discovery of finding both rough stones and jewels. It often is a slow and energy-consuming process of struggling with just the right mix of mechanics and content to create something new, a twist of human thought and feeling and action not quite seen or heard or felt before—and also probably never again. The promise of entry into this behind-the-scenes drama is what entices young writers to struggle again and again with certain mechanics, to persevere when things aren't sounding right, to keep trying even though they feel they have little or nothing to say, and to continue to look for and find small ways to link content and mechanics. As the writer Barry Hannah (2010) observed, "language still strikes me as a miracle, a thing the deepest mind adores." For young writers, this happens here and there in moments of placing just the right letter or word or feeling or object in just the right place at just the right time in just the right way. When this happens, and it does not often happen in a linear way but in a more stop-start and back-and-forth way, young writers experience a moment of a writing and language "miracle" and touch something that the "deepest" writing "mind adores."

For many young writers, the motivation to meld content and mechanics comes about through the attractive pull of originality and creativity. This force, though, must come from somewhere, and it comes from our inventive and yet structured opportunities to plan, compose, and revise. Most young writers only "buy into" the allure of originality and creativity when they sense and see their own progress, their own moving forward, small signposts that show they can orchestrate elements of mechanics and content in accurate and pleasurable ways. When we support and guide young writers, bit by bit and often in baby steps, they begin to see the wide-open possibilities for melding content and mechanics. The poet Robert Creeley has remarked on the sense of limitlessness that can accompany writing well.

If at times that I have said that I enjoy what I write, I mean that writing is for me the most viable and open condition of possibility in the world. Things have happened there, as they have happened nowhere else—and I am not speaking of "make-believe," which, be it said, is "as real as real can be." In poems I have discovered and borne testament to my life in ways no other possibility has given me. (quoted in Friedlander, 2008, p. 4)

The bit-by-bit accumulation and layering of content and mechanics integration slowly affirms for children who they are and what they might be as young writers. As Anne Haas Dyson (1986, 1989, 1993, 2003) has shown, children write themselves and others into their stories and poems and other pieces of writing. They become themselves as they become writers. They also learn to see where they can make a place for themselves as social and intellectual actors in and out of the classroom. The children's book author and illustrator Grace Lin ("Why Couldn't Snow White Be Chinese," n.d.) writes about her childhood yearning for her cultural identity and sense of self to be reflected and included in the pantheon of children's books.

The books that I loved and read did not help me answer that question. Betsy and Billy were nice friends but they didn't understand. Neither did Madeline, Eloise, or Mike Mulligan. Cinderella, Snow White? I didn't even try to explain. Rikki Tikki Tembo and Five Chinese Brothers tried to be pals, but really what did we have in common?

Nothing. And so I remained different from my friends in real life, different from my fictional friends in stories . . . somehow always different. (online)

When young writers discover bits and pieces of originality and creativity, they begin to "understand" their own place in relation to their written texts. They meld content and mechanics with just enough accuracy and flair that they don't "need to explain" what their texts are and who they speak for. Their writing speaks for itself. Writing well demands, even for young writers in the K–4 span, that they learn to see that they have "something in common" with all the existing texts and genres out there that they read and talk about, and also "something in common" with the new texts they create through writing. And while young writers may at times "remain different" from "fictional friends," the originality and creativity of their writing allows them to create new fictional friends who are like them and speak for them. Young writers learn to do this through melding content and mechanics in accurate and creative ways, which contributes to an increasingly sophisticated writing mind.

THE EVOLVING TEACHING MIND

As educators, our writing mind is only as strong as our teaching mind. And yet the two complement and nurture each other. The teachers featured in this book have increased my own understanding of the complexities of integrating content and mechanics in the teaching of writing to young writers. I now see more clearly the depth of challenges and rewards that a focus on this integration can be for young writers and for ourselves as teachers. When I envisioned this book, and thought about talking with the seven teachers, I anticipated a more clear-cut and isolated focus on content and mechanics. I was pleasantly surprised to hear the teachers speak of a more nuanced, more embedded, view of written language content and mechanics more closely tied to individual children's talents and needs, children's overall language and literacy development, the demands of learning to write in a new language, the power of linking writing with reading, and other high-level and sophisticated ideas.

If we are to progress as teachers of writing, and as researchers of how we can teach children to write well, we need to reaffirm the importance of knowledge and ideas. This is both a pedagogical and a policy and political matter. As discussed in Chapter 1, we have 40 years of wonderful research and theory to add onto and extend. This is the time for us to move forward to increasingly sophisticated ideas and knowledge about how children learn to write well—and for the focus of this book, how we can envision and teach content and mechanics integration. A continued overemphasis on low-level mechanics at the expense of mechanics and content integration, and a continued emphasis on not nurturing our teaching minds, only serve to impede our individual and collective knowledge of what works well for us and our children. It is the growth of ideas—big ones and small ones—that provides new possibilities and strategies for supporting and guiding children to write well.

The teachers featured in this book remind themselves of certain ideas and experiences to maintain their passion and skill in teaching writing. Florence Tse, who teaches kindergarten, looks at the daily writing of her students as a source of passion and engagement in teaching writing.

> One of my students wrote me a letter about their day. It's one sentence. A lot of my students don't get support at home and to see them write at this level is tremendously rewarding, not only as their teacher but I think for themselves that they feel really good about themselves. They are trying their best and excelling.
>
> This is how I stay passionate and engaged in teaching writing. Also, empowering young children to document and publish their work is very rewarding. They identify themselves as writers, as authors, and as illustrators.

For Ilsa Miller, in 1st grade, writing with her students keeps her engaged with her students and her writing instruction.

Writing with my students helps keep me interested and helps improve my own writing and my own reading. When I'm reading certain things, I often say to myself, "This would be great to show the children," even if one sentence can make a difference for them because that's what is most applicable to 1st-graders. Everything I read makes me think about writing and how to teach it and how to interest the students. I also stay passionate about teaching when I see the children's reactions when I publish their writing, especially when I help them make it into a cloth book. They're so excited to share it with their parents, their buddy class, and the other 1st-grade class.

Jim Gray (2000) argues that writing on our own and with students renews the writing spirit and our inner drive as teachers of writing.

These teachers [in the National Writing Project], lured into the chance to spend time writing together, know the great secret: a writer is the opposite of a piece of chalk—the more you write, the bigger you become. Just as these teachers are more interested in what their own students can do than what they can absorb, these teachers want to know how they can express, discover, and surprise themselves by writing. They went into teaching because they loved to read and write, and now they find themselves with precious little time to do either. (p. 88)

Amanda Abarbanel-Rice gains motivation and insight from observation and reflection on her own reading and writing, and sharing her insights with her 2nd-grade students.

I draw on my experiences as a reader and writer. When I am writing during our mini-lessons, I get ideas. When I practice and experience a certain genre as a writer, I understand it better. I try to articulate out loud to the class whatever insights I am having about that genre. Good writing involves working out questions *as* we are writing. I try to do a lot of metacognition for myself and also with the goal of students doing it for themselves.

Liz Goss, another 2nd-grade teacher, gains inspiration from contributing to her students' writing success and achievements.

I become passionate about my children's writing when I see their language and writing capturing their imagination and their interests. The writing that they are capable of when given the correct tools and time is amazing. I rarely had a chance to put my ideas on paper in a creative or critical way until college. I am so excited about how my students are creating different genres of writing and know the power of their own voice. I am also fascinated by how their personalities and identities come out in their writing. Writing allows me to treat each child as a full human being, capable of expressing their understanding of the complexity of their world.

Having few memories of writing well as a student in her K–12 education, Liz prizes a "creative and critical" approach to teaching writing for her students. It provides a vision and a philosophy that writing well allows children to create their own genres, "create their own voice," and for Liz to relate to each student as "full human being."

Madhuvanti Khare, teaching 3rd grade, also believes in the value of writing on her own, both in and outside of her classroom, and of the continual cultivation of new ideas about teaching children to write well.

> Unless you write, it's really hard to think about teaching writing. I think this is especially true for some of the more creative writing. A lot of us learn to write nonfiction writing in college but not creative writing. So I write with my students, and I also write with my own children at home. I also stay passionate about teaching writing by thinking about and trying to understand children's struggles with writing. I often wonder why something is difficult for them and what kind of scaffolding I can provide for the next child who's going to have that struggle.

Madhuvanti, like the other teachers featured in this book, values her own writing as a way to keep pace with the demands and challenges that her students face.

Sarah Carp, teaching 4th grade, finds motivation to teach writing and to teach it well through her own reading and discovering what motivates her students to write.

> I love looking at my students' work and thinking about what I want to do next and what they need. For instance, I recently noticed that my students are writing with sentences such as "I'm going to talk about this" and "If you want to read this paragraph keep going," and I'm trying to figure out what kind of stylistic lessons I need to teach to help the students move away from this style. Writing lends itself to focusing on individual children because it is self-differentiated, and I become passionate about teaching writing when I see my students' feelings of pride and excitement about their writing. All students want to express themselves and so the opportunities to write, document their lives, and share their writing with others is

often very motivating. I am also motivated when I can connect my students' writing to their reading—my teaching then has a sense of completeness and wholeness.

For Sarah, tailoring her teaching to each child's writing is a source of motivation, as is sharing her students' "feeling of price and excitement" in their writing. Sarah also remains passionate about teaching writing by sharing her students' motivation and drive to "write, document their lives, and share it with others."

———————————

Emilia Ferreiro (2003) notes that we "are witness to a new aesthetic fragmentation, a sort of 'aesthetic of fragmentation'" where "the criteria for a 'well-structured' text" might need to change (p. 51). In this book, we've looked at new ideas and tools for understanding and teaching the integration of content and mechanics in the writing of young authors. The teachers featured in this book have shared their philosophies and strategies for supporting and guiding young writers toward an increasingly accurate and effective integration of these two elements of writing well. Their work, as well as the other ideas presented here, serve us well as we ponder what Ferreiro's "well-structured text" might mean for us and for our particular students. As much as we might be asked to teach only certain texts according to policy documents and writing standards, we need to seek and teach a wide variety of texts that integrate meaning and mechanics. Ultimately, and this can mean starting tomorrow, we must gain control over what constitutes our writing and teaching mind.

In "Reserved" (2007), the poet Rae Armantrout writes:

> Narrative prepares me
> to see
> what I see next.
>
> Not getting lost
> but looping
> then extending myself
>
> afresh
> starburst,
>
> reversing myself
> as if turning
> to face a partner

Writing well, and teaching writing, are a lot like Armantrout's "narrative prepares me/to see/what I see next." We go forward when we teach children to write well bit by bit, narrative step by narrative step. We are beholden to our own developing understanding of what it means to write well and how to teach it, and we are beholden to children's own developmental leaps as well as starts and stops. Neither one of us can get ahead of ourselves and each other. We can only plan for now and wait and see "what I [we] see next." And what we see next in teaching children to write well has a lot do with how we envision and teach children to integrate content and mechanics. This direction is ever-changing—thankfully and yet frustratingly—and it often means "looping/then extending myself [ourselves]" and "reversing myself [ourselves]/as if turning/to face a partner." The "partner" is both our evolving understanding of what it means to write well and our evolving toolbox of strategies to help young writers meld content and mechanics in their writing. It is my hope that this book has contributed to a greater understanding of the role of this "partner," and how the reading of this book is another "looping" and "extending" step along our path as writers and teachers.

REFERENCES

Ada, A. F. (1995). *My name is Maria Isabel*. New York: Aladdin Books.

Ada, A. F. (n.d.). A bilingual author. Retrieved July 28, 2010, from http://www.colorincolorado.org/read/meet/ada/transcript#process

Archambault, J., & Martin, B. (1989). *Chicka chicka boom boom*. New York: Simon & Schuster.

Armantrout, R. (2007). *Next life*. Middletown, CT: Wesleyan University Press.

Atwell, N. (1987). *In the middle: Writing, reading, and learning with adolescents*. Portsmouth, NH: Heinemann.

Bissex, G. (1980). *GNYS at WRK: A child learns to write and read*. Cambridge, MA: Harvard University Press.

Bissex, G. (1996). *Partial truths: A memoir and essays on reading, writing, and research*. Portsmouth, NH: Heinemann.

Blackal, S., & Burrows, A. (2007). *Ivy and Bean*. San Francisco: Chronicle Books.

Britton, J. (1970). The student's writing. In E. L. Evertts (Ed.), *Explorations in children's writing* (pp. 21–65). Champaign, IL: National Council of Teachers of English.

Britton, J. (1982). *Prospect and retrospect: Selected essays of James Britton*. (Ed. Gordon M. Pradl). Montclair, NJ: Boynton/Cook.

Britton, J. (1982). Spectator role and the beginning of writing. In M. Nystrand (Ed.), *What writers know: The language, process, and structure of written discourse*. New York: Academic Press.

Britton, J. (1983). Writing and the story world. In B. M. Kroll & G. Wells (Eds.), *Explorations in the development of writing* (pp. 3–30). London: John Wiley & Sons.

Britton, J. (1987). Vygotsky's contribution to pedagogical theory. *English Education, 21*, 22–26.

California Department of Education. (1998). *English-language arts content standards for California public schools: Kindergarten through grade twelve*. Sacramento, CA: Author.

Calkins, L. M. (1986). *The art of teaching writing*. Portsmouth, NH: Heinemann.

Calkins, L. M. (2003). *Units of study for primary writing: A yearlong curriculum*. Portsmouth, NH: Heinemann.

Calkins, L. M. (2006). *Units of study for teaching writing: Grades 3–5*. Portsmouth, NH: Heinemann.

Cambourne, B., & Turbill, J. (1987). *Coping with chaos*. Rozelle, NSW, Australia: Primary English Teaching Association.

Carlson, N. (1994). *How to lose all your friends*. New York: Puffin.

Cazden, C. (1988). *Classroom discourse*. Portsmouth, NH: Heinemann.

Child, L. (2000). *I will not ever eat a tomato*. Cambridge, MA: Candlewick Press.

Chomsky, C. (1970). Reading, writing, and phonology. *Harvard Educational Review, 40*, 287–309.

Chomsky, C. (1971). Write first, read later. *Childhood Education, 47*(6), 296–299.

Clay, M. (1975). *What did I write?* Auckland, New Zealand: Heinemann.

Clay, M. (1998). *By different paths to common outcomes*. Auckland: Heinemann.

Clay, M. (2005). *An observation survey of early literacy achievement, 2nd Edition*. York, ME: Stenhouse.

Coleridge, S. (1985). *Biographia literaria*. Princeton, NJ: Princeton University Press.

Dahl, R. (1988). *Matilda*. New York: Scholastic.

Delpit, L. (1986). Skills and other dilemmas of a progressive black educator. *Harvard Educational Review, 56*(4), 379–386.

Delpit, L. (1988). The silenced dialogue: Power and pedagogy in educating other people's children. *Harvard Educational Review, 58*(3), 280–298.

Delpit, L. (1998). *Other people's children: Cultural conflict in the classroom*. New York: The New Press.

Delpit, L. (2002). No kinda sense. In L. Delpit & J. K. Dowdy (Eds.), *The skin that we speak: Thoughts on language and culture in the classroom* (pp. 33–48). New York: New Press.

DiCamillo, K. (2009). *Mercy Watson*. Cambridge, MA: Candlewick Press.

Dixon, J. (1967). *Growth through English*. Reading, England: National Association for the Teaching of English.

Dixon, J., & Stratta, S. (1986). *Writing narrative—and beyond*. Ottawa, Canada: Canadian Council of Teachers.

Dorn, L., & Soffos, C. (2001). *Scaffolding young writers: A writers' workshop approach*. Portland, ME: Stenhouse.

Dyson, A. H. (1986). Staying free to dance with the children: The dangers of sanctifying activities in the language arts curriculum. *English Education, 18*(3), 135–146.

Dyson, A. H. (1989). *Multiple worlds of child writers: Friends learning to write*. New York: Teachers College Press.

Dyson, A. H. (1993). *Social worlds of children learning to write in an urban school*. New York: Teachers College Press.

Dyson, A. H. (2000). Writing and the sea of voices: Oral language in, around, and about writing. In R. Indrisano & J. R. Squire (Eds.), *Perspectives on writing: Research, theory, and practice* (pp. 45–65). Newark, DE: International Reading Association.

Dyson, A. H. (2003). *The brothers and sisters learn to write: Popular literacies in childhood and school cultures*. New York: Teachers College Press.

Dyson, A. H., & Genishi, C. (1994). *The need for story: Cultural diversity in classroom and community*. Urbana, IL: National Council of Teachers of English.

Dyson, A. H., & Genishi, C. (2009). *Children, language, and literacy: Diverse learners in diverse times*. New York: Teachers College Press.

Emig, J. (1983). *The web of meaning: Essays on writing, teaching, learning, and thinking*. Upper Montclair, NJ: Boynton/Cook.

Ferreiro, E. (2003). *Essays on literacy: Past and present of the verbs to read and to write*. Toronto: Groundwood.

Ferreiro, E., & Teberosky, A. (1982). *Literacy before schooling*. Portsmouth, NH: Heinemann.

Frere-Jones, S. (2010, March 8). As is: Bill Withers makes no apologies. *The New Yorker*, 76–77.

Friedlander, B. (Ed.). (2008). *Robert Creeley, Selected poems (1945–2005)*. Berkeley, CA: University of California Press.

Glover, M. (2009). *Engaging young writers: Preschool–grade 1*. Portsmouth, NH: Heinemann.

Graves, D. (1983). *Writing: Teachers & children at work*. Exeter, NH: Heinemann.

Graves, D. (1994). *A fresh look at writing*. Portsmouth, NH: Heinemann.

Gray, J. (2000). *Teachers at the center: A memoir of the early years of the National Writing Project*. Berkeley, CA: National Writing Project.

Gregory, E. (2001). Sisters and brothers as language and literacy teachers: Synergy between siblings playing and working together. *Journal of Early Literacy, 1*(3), 301–322.

Gregory, E. (2008). *Learning to read in a new language*. London: Sage Publications.

Guthrie, J. (2009). *Vendela Vida wraps trilogy on women in crisis. San Francisco Chronicle*, p. E8.

Hannah, B. (2010, June). Why I write. *Harper's Magazine*, 16.

Heald-Taylor, G. (1986). *Whole language strategies for ESL students*. Toronto: Ontario Institute for Studies in Education.

Henkes, K. (1997). *Chester's way*. New York: Greenwillow.

Kasza, K. (1996). *The wolf's chicken stew*. New York: Putnam.

Koch, N. (2005). Different water. *River of words* (p. 36). Berkeley, CA: River of Words.

Ladson-Billings, G. (2002). I ain't writin' nuttin': Permissions to fail and demands to succeed in urban classrooms. In L. Delpit & J. K. Dowdy (Eds.), *The skin that we speak: Thoughts on language and culture in the classroom* (pp. 109–120). New York: New Press.

Lahr, J. (2010, May 3). Master of revels: Neil Simon's comic empire. *The New Yorker*, 72–76.

Lin, G. (n.d.). The extra adjective: How I came to terms with being a multicultural book author. Retrieved July 28, 2010, from http://www.gracelin.com/media/press/press.extrajdessay.pdf

Lin, G. (n.d.). Why couldn't Snow White be Chinese? Finding identity through children's books. Retrieved September 14, 2010, from http://www.gracelin.com/media/press/press_snowwhiteessay.pdf

Loer, S. (n.d.). An interview with Allen Say. Retrieved July 13, 2010, from http://www.hmhbooks.com/authors/allensay/questions.shtml

Low, D. (2010). Conversations: A remarkable literary debut. *Wesleyan, 1*, 16.

Macrorie, K. (1984). *Writing to be read* (3rd ed.). Upper Montclair, NJ: Boynton/Cook.

Martin, N., & Milford, J. (1971). Spelling etc. In A. Jones & J. Mulford (Eds.), *Children using language: An approach to English in the primary school* (pp. 153–174). Oxford, England: Oxford University Press.

Meier, D. (1988). Moments of voice in the writing of young children. *English in Education*, 22(2), 36–41.

Mermelstein, L. (2006). *Reading/writing connections in the K–2 classroom*. New York: Pearson.

Metselaar, M. & van der Rol, R. (2004). *Anne Frank: Her life in words and pictures from the archives of the Anne Frank house*. New York: Roaring Brook Press.

Miller, D. (2002). *Reading with meaning: Teaching comprehension in the primary grades*. Portland, ME: Stenhouse.

Moffett, J. (1988). *Coming on center: Essays in English education* (2nd ed.). Portsmouth, NH: Heinemann.

Moss, M. (2006). *Amelia's notebook*. New York: Simon & Schuster.

The New Yorker. (2010, June 14 & 21). Comment: 20 under 40, 49–50.

Peterson, R. T. (2006). *From all things considered: My birding adventures*. New York: Houghton Mifflin.

Pinkney, A. D. (1999). *Duke Ellington: The piano prince and his orchestra*. New York: Hyperion.

Ray, K. W. (1999). *Wondrous words: Writers and writing in the elementary classroom*. Urbana, IL: National Council of Teachers of English.

Read, C. (1971). Preschool children's knowledge of English phonology. *Harvard Educational Review*, 41(1), 1–34.

Read, C. (1981). Writing is not the inverse of reading. In C. H. Frederiksen & J. F. Dominic (Eds.), *Writing: The nature, development and teaching of written communication* (pp. 105–118). [Vol. 2 in series Writing: Process, development, and communication]. Lawrence, NJ: Earlbaum.

Reyes, M. de la Luz. (1992). Challenging venerable assumptions: Literacy instruction for linguistically different students. *Harvard Educational Review*, 62(4), 427–446.

Richgels, D. J. (2001). Invented spelling, phonemic awareness, and reading and writing instruction. In S. B. Neuman & D. Dickinson (Eds.), *Handbook of early literacy research* (pp. 142–155). New York: Guilford Press.

Samway, K. D. (2006). *When English learners write: Connecting research to practice, K–8*. Portsmouth, NH: Heinemann.

Stribling, S. M., & Kraus, S. M. (2007). Content and mechanics: Understanding first grade writers. *Voices of Practitioners*, 1–17.

Stubbs, M. (2002). Some basic sociolinguistic concepts. In L. Delpit & J. K. Dowdy (Eds.), *The skin that we speak: Thoughts on language and culture in the classroom* (pp. 65–85). New York: New Press.

Vygotsky, L. S. (1978). *Mind in society*. Cambridge, MA: Harvard University Press.

Vygotsky, L. S. (1986). *Thought and language*. Cambridge, MA: MIT Press.

Williams, S. (1996). *I went walking*. New York: Harcourt Brace.

Woolf, V. *A writer's diary*. London: Harcourt Brace.

Yolen, J. (1987). *Owl moon*. New York: Penguin.

INDEX

Abarbanel-Rice, Amanda, 10, 42, 85
Abbreviation principles, 23
Abstractions, 20
Access, 7, 25, 77
Accountability, 110
Accuracy, 2, 3, 4, 108
Active learners, 24
Ada, Alma Flor, 105
Aesthetic of fragmentation, 78
African American children, 26, 40, 106, 109–110
Alliterative effect, 2
Ambition, 79, 136
Amelia's Notebook (Moss), 75
Anticipation, 3, 94
Appropriate adaptation, 95
Archambault, J., 117
Armantrout, Rae, 142
Asking questions, 45
Assessment, 4
Assigning sound value to letters, 21
Atwell, Nancie, 65, 93
Audience, 3, 6, 9, 25, 69, 87
Authentic experiences, 108
Authorship, 41, 46, 80, 86, 104

Background knowledge, 3, 53, 54, 75
Bakhtin, 28
Balance of content and mechanics, 22
Basic elements of written language, 47
Basic principles for early writing, 58
Basic skills, 4, 27, 33, 35, 40, 65

Beginning-middle-end structure, 69, 72, 73
Bissex, G., 8, 18, 19, 113
Book reviews, 49, 131
Breaking down elements of written conventions, 39
Breaking down language, 5
Breaking down texts, 88
Bridge between two-dimensional (drawing), 58
Bridge to three-dimensional space (real life), 58
Britton, James, 15–16, 41, 48, 57, 58, 91, 92, 94, 103, 104, 107. *See also* Internalization; Shaping at the point of utterance; Vygotsky, Lev; Zone of proximal development
Building up texts, 88

California English–Language Arts Content Standards, 33
Calkins, Lucy, 25, 43, 44, 45, 61, 64, 86, 92–93, 95–96, 115, 117. *See also* Authorship; *Firsthand* curriculum; Mini lessons; Relationship between reading and writing; Story mountain; Units of study curriculum; Writer's workshops
Cambourne, B., 18
Carp, Sarah, 11, 48, 54, 130
Cazden, Courtney, 15, 27, 108

Certainty of language, 88–89
Changes in society and human action, 8
Challenges
  children as manipulators of
      boundaries and tensions, 28
  in content, 55
  differentiated and individualized, 48
  between form and content, 52
  and high-level tasks, 29
  in mechanics, 55
  teachers and children, 25
  in writing, 54
Chester's Way (Henkes), 91
Chicka Chicka Boom Boom
    (Archambault & Martin), 117
Child mind, 8. *See also* Teaching mind;
    Writing mind
Children of color, 26, 53
Children as "real writers," 24
Children's identities as writers and
    learners, 64
Children's interests, 24, 36, 66, 115
Children's perspectives, 28, 35
Children's sociocultural talents and
    traditions, 28
Chinese, 37, 54, 84
Chomsky, Carol, 18–19, 24
Choosing topics, 64
Chronological history, 13
Chunks of language, 65, 73, 83, 90,
    108–109. *See also* Gregory, Eve
Clay, Marie, 21, 24, 41, 45, 58, 85 *See
    also* Relationship between reading
    and writing; Six principles of
    writing and drawing
Code-switch, 109
Cognition, 17, 21, 30, 49, 52, 57
Coleridge, Samuel, 81
Collaboration, 93
Commitment to students, 79
Communication, 24, 28, 35, 57, 64,
    83, 88

Community
  based ways, 30
  collaborative learning, 30
  and education, 107
  group consciousness, 25
  learning, 53
  of writers, talkers, and thinkers, 16
  of writers in domain, 27
  of writers and thinkers, 4
  and writing, 28
  writing for, 107
Completing a research project, 76
Composing, 79–80
  building blocks for effective
      composing, 95
  built-in power of composing, 81
  content and mechanics, 79
  as drama, 81
  dual-language composure, 117–119
  and editing, 120–121
  elements, 84
  an experience, 88
  and feelings, 81
  more than once in each genre, 93
  as more than writing, 80
  music, 79
  philosophy and strategies, 81, 86
Computer writing, 108–109
Confidence, 6, 66, 79, 84, 89, 107
Connection to writing behaviors, 24
Constructivist learning theories, 37
Content. *See also* Content and
    mechanics integration; Content to
    mechanics ratio; Mechanics
  adopting new voices, 49
  children's focus on, 36
  as deepening and broadening writing,
      43
  engaging, 83
  as intangible, 6
  as malleable elements, 4
  and meaning, 32, 37

preparing children, 49
recognizable and patterned language, 82
Content and mechanics integration,
    1, 2, 35, 90. *See also* Content;
    Content to mechanics ratio;
    Mechanic
balanced with needs of students, 130
as children write, 43
children's internal balance, 40
conventions and meaning, 8
dance, 87
in editing and revision, 103
final phase, 100
within genres, 95
inseparable and closely aligned, 7
mixing and matching in editing, 130
peer editing checklist, 112
reading stories aloud, 130
reflection and awareness, 85
in social studies and science projects,
    45
style and tone in mechanics and
    content, 51
word choice, 89, 132–133
writing well, 135
Content to mechanics ratio, 9, 85
Contrastive Principle, 22–23
Control for young writers, 4–5, 15
Conventions, 4, 48. *See also* Mechanics
of language, 2
of print, 48
of spelling, 2, 20, 22
as tangibles, 6
understanding, 36, 64
Conversation, 58, 117, 119–120,
    130–131
Converting language into an object of
    thought, 86
Cooperative behavior, 58
Correctness, 20, 40
Creative writing, 22
Creeley, Robert, 137

Cultural knowledge, 30, 54
biological knowledge 18
clash between home and school, 27
conventions expected in community, 27
and linguistic factors for pedagogy
    and instruction, 29
routines around literacy, 30
routines in home and community, 54
and social traditions, 16
Culture of mechanics, 42
Culture of writing, 8
Cultures, codes, and contexts, 21, 26,
    30, 105–106
Curriculum, 4, 99

Dahl, Roald, 131–133, 137
Daily oral language, 108
Daily routines, 3
Defining content and mechanics, 32
Delpit, Lisa, 26, 53, 64, 79, 99,
    105–106, 108, 110, 135–136. *See
    also* African American children;
    Community; Expert knowledge;
    Potential brilliance; Support for
    young writers
Desire to be great, 6
Development of young children, 14, 42,
    54, 65
Developmental regression in mechanics,
    84, 85
Developmentally appropriate support,
    7, 38, 41, 92
DiCamillo, K., 91
Dictation, 2
Different social structures, 22
Direct explicit instruction, 83
Direct guidance, 7, 53, 64, 66
Direct opportunities, 7
Directional Principle, 22–23
Diversity within literacy, 22
Dixon, John, 69, 88
Dorn, Linda, 112

Drawing
  with intentionality, 59
  linking ideas, feelings, and images
      with words, 58
  linking written text, 60
  and scaffolding, 61
  talking, and writing planning
      resources, 57
  as a way to "say" things, 60
Dual approach, 27
Duke Ellington (Pinkney & Pinkney),
  51
Dynamic and interwoven relationship, 6
Dyson, Anne Haas, 26, 27, 28, 44, 53,
      104–105, 138. *See also* Content
      and mechanics integration

Editing and revising, 100, 133
  challenges for students, 100
  challenges for teachers, 101
  computers, 108–109
  conversation, 117, 119–120
  editing toolbox, 100
  editors in chief, 112
  front-loading revision, 121
  learning, 113
  one-on-one conferences, 120–123
  over-editing, 50, 132
  peer editing, 110–112
  strategies, 106
  theoretical foundations, 101
Educational philosophy, 8, 10, 32
ELD classroom, 38
Elements of writing
  mechanics and elements of meaning, 8
  mechanics and orchestration, 61–62
  in mentor texts, 44
  narrative through reading and
      discussion, 44
  sentence frames, 83
  style, 5
Embed writing in classroom life, 53
Emig, Janet, 58

Endurance, 107–108
Engaging students through literacy, 40,
  45, 69
English, 29
English Language Learners, 89. *See also*
  New language learners
Entry points into writing, 73
Experiences and writing, 9, 28, 31, 69, 90
Expert knowledge, 26, 53, 135
External beauty of written work, 79,
  103. *See also* Internal beauty of
  written work
External speech, 59

False dichotomy, 4
Familiarity with stories, 44
Ferreiro, Emilia, 21, 22, 40, 78, 85, 95,
  142
Fictional friends, 138
First act or drafts, 81
First grade, 39
First teaching place, 82
Firsthand curriculum, 80, 92
Five levels that indicate growth, 21
Flair, voice, and passion, 4, 139
Fluency, 4, 27, 41
Focus on structure and process, 26
Focused opportunities, 2, 3
Font and center mechanics, 42
Form over content, 33
Formation of letters, 2, 5
Found objects, 61
Foundations of early literacy, 4, 7, 50, 57
Four effects on reading from writing, 23
Four essential elements of narrative
  writing, 69
Fourth grade, 48
Frank, Anne, 6
Freedom of children and teachers, 3, 32
Friedlander, B., 138
Frere-Jones, S., 81
Freshness of perspective, 78
Front-loading revision, 121

Full-fledged authoring, 79, 80
Future roadblocks, 52

Generating Principle, 22, 23
Genishi, C., 44
Genres, 44, 75, 76, 78, 92
    that complement one another, 92
    forms of written language, 94
    mechanics and content, 47
    particulars, 95
    and personal story, 104
    read alouds, 48
    reading with composing, 81
    reflection on content, 86
    and student's voice, 140–141
    study of different genres, 46, 47
    written language formats, 5
    zone of proximal development, 48
Global understanding of language, 21
Glover, M., 73
Go forward, 104
Goal of writing, 2, 107
Gordon, Joli, 11, 43, 75
Goss, Liz, 10, 40, 106
Grade-level expectations, 34, 101, 112
Gradual release from teacher modeling, 83
Graves, Donald, 24, 63, 64, 79, 93 101,
    113, 116
Gray, James, 86, 140
Gregory, Eve, 3, 30, 44, 47, 48, 54,
    64, 65, 73, 75, 76, 82, 83, 90, 96,
    99. See also Cultural knowledge;
    Inside-out approach; New
    language learners; Outside-in
    approach
Gross approximations, 22
Growth of ideas, 139
Guided instruction, 64
Guided participation, 30
Guthrie, J., 53

Habit of mind, 42
Habit of practice, 42

Hannah, Barry, 137
Heald-Taylor, G., 29
Henkes, K., 91
Home-school connections, 30
    cultural traditions of language and
        literacy, 7
How and why we teach writing, 5
How to Lose All Your Friends
    (Carlson), 91
How-to writing, 2–3
Human eye to plan, compose, and
    revise, 59

I Went Walking (Williams), 83
I Will Not Ever Eat a Tomato (Child), 84
Importance of form, 29
Importance of the process of writing, 54
Independent learners, 23, 83
Indirect guidance, 7
Indirect opportunities, 7
Individual needs of students, 28, 33,
    46–47, 49, 54, 113, 119–120
Informal learning situations, 30
Initiation into a new culture, 31
Inner speech, 15, 80, 94
Inquiry, 45
Inside-out approach, 30, 38, 47, 48, 54,
    65, 90, 99. See also Gregory, Eve;
    Outside-in approach
Inspiration, 3, 6, 79
Interactive writing, 38, 73, 75
Internal beauty of written work, 103.
    See also External beauty of written
    work
Internalization, 16–17
International look at literacy, 21
Interplay between multiple worlds, 28
Inventive language and action, 2
Inventory Principle, 22, 23
Ivy and Bean (Blackal & Burrows), 90

Joyful writing experiences, 95
Jumping off point for writing, 84

Key elements of integration, 4–5
Khare, Madhuvanti, 11, 43, 92, 120
Kindergarten, 38, 59, 73
Knowledge
  and articulation, 5
  of experiences, 31, 58
  of language forms, 53
  versus novelty, 22
  of personal strengths, 6
  of powerful teaching, 5
  of powerful writing, 5
  of a set of rules, 26
  of word meanings, 5
Kraus, Susan, 35, 85

Ladson-Billings, G., 79
Lahr, J., 5
Language and music, 135
Language as a miracle, 137
Larger text forms, 65
Learning mind, 135
Learning to love writing, 7, 41
Letter sets, 19
Levels of meaning, 2
Levels of simultaneity, 80
Lifelong habits, 3
Lin, Grace, 104, 138
Linguistic innovation, 78
Listening to the ideas of others, 7
Literacy policy, 4, 33
Literacy programs/models, 19
Loer, S., 61
Low, D., 53
Luscious language and wonderful
    words, 89, 90, 92

Macrorie, Ken, 52, 79
Making marks and symbols, 58
Making meaning through writing, 37
Manipulating language, 23
Martin, B., 117
Martin, Nancy, 33–34
Matilda (Dahl), 131–133, 137

Mechanics. See also Content; Content
    and mechanics integration;
    Content to mechanics ratio
  attention to, 108
  awareness of, 25, 38
  as children are writing, 43
  control over, 2
  and conventions, 32, 36
  editing process, 39
  elements of, 90
  inter-sentence, 63
  intra-sentence, 63
  masses of detail, 136
  moving away from tradition, 51
  as "nuts and bolts" of writing, 41, 46
  orchestration, 61
  as part of planning, 66
  quantifiable, 134
  as quantifiable for children, 6
  solid foundation, 4
  as tangible, 33
  that can be reread by peer, 39
Meier, D., 44
Memoir/personal narrative, 46, 47, 76,
    96, 141–142
Mental images, 87, 88
Mentor texts, 44, 47, 48, 114
Mercy Watson (DiCamillo), 91
Mermelstein, Leah, 44, 73, 75, 76
Metalanguage, 85
Metselaar, M., 6
Middle ground, 116
Miller, D., 83, 88, 116
Miller, Ilsa, 10, 39, 65
Mini lessons, 43, 45–46, 64–65, 77, 87,
    91, 93. See also Calkins, Lucy
Moffett, James, 33, 79, 80, 99, 104
Moment by moment process, 94
Moments of voice, 81
Momentum, 4
Moss, M., 75
Motivation, 4, 6, 50, 75, 106, 137,
    139–143

Moving beyond a monolithic path, 27
Mulford, Jeremy, 33–34
My Name Is María Isabal (Ada), 97

Natural storytelling process, 61
New language learners, 2–3, 28–30, 37,
    50, 54, 64, 66. *See also* Gregory,
    Eve; Delpit, Lisa.
    balance of mechanics and content, 130
    benefits from reading aloud, 95
    direct support and guidance for, 83, 99
    editing and revision, 101, 105, 115
    linking reading and writing, 95
    mini lessons, 65
    modifications, 29
    previewing elements, 95
    receptive language, 95
    strategies, 66
    transferring knowledge, 5
    vocabulary, 64
    writing strategies, 29
New Yorker, The, 78
Nonfiction pieces, 43
Not to get stuck, 6

Observation and analysis of product, 24
One-on-one composing, 84
One-on-one conferences, 120
Open opportunities, 2–3
Oral and written language, 5, 94
Oral language, 22, 24, 27–28, 30, 73
Organization of thoughts, 64
Originality (creativity), 2–4, 36,
    136–138
Outside-in approach, 30, 44, 47, 54,
    65, 73, 75, 76, 83, 90, 96, 99.
    See also Gregory, Eve; Inside-out
    approach
Owl Moon (Yolen), 89–90

Parallel linguistic process, 59
Parameters of content and mechanics, 78
Patterns, 18, 61, 82

Peer culture, 104–105
Peer editing, 39, 43
    checklists, 110–112
    pairing students, 114
    and peer culture, 105
    role of peers and response, 24–25
    support and responses, 41, 54, 84
Peterson, Roger Tory, 135–136
Phonics, 18–19
Piagetian perspective, 21
Picture books, 96, 97
Pictures, 61
Pinkney, Andrea Davis, 51
Pinkney, Brian, 51
Planning, 52
    as actual writing, 52, 77
    and choosing content, 63
    and composing with students, 69
    dance with composure, 57
    effective, 64
    flexibility, 52
    peer collaboration, 60
    the process, 75
    process time varies, 53
    real-life model, 73
    sense of responsibility for, 64
    sheet for editing mechanics and
        content, 73
    stretching writing possibilities, 57
Poetry, 46–47, 109
Post-it visuals, 96, 97, 98
Potential brilliance, 79, 99, 136
Potential content and potential
    mechanics, 94
Power
    in classroom, 27
    images and visualization, 87–88
    of language, 16
    linking reading and writing, 43
    of reading ahead, 95
    of story, 44, 52
    of writing, 4, 35
    of the written word, 8

Predictable format, 38
Prehistory of written language, 14
Premeditation, 103
Presentation, 35
Print in environment, 29
Prompts and frames, 81–82, 92
Publishing writing, 24, 104, 110–112
Purpose of text, 75

Questions and possible answers, 84
Quick-writes, 45–46

Raw materials, 37, 46
Read, Charles, 18, 24
Read-alouds, 73, 84, 94–96
Reader's workshop, 73
Reading and listening critically, 95
Reading and responding by peers, 93
Reading with purpose, 20
Reflection and awareness, 81, 85, 86,
    91, 99
  in editing, 103
  of language, 45, 58
  of stories, 45
  of strengths, 6
  of thought process, 103
  of wider world, 28
  of work, 39
Reflective teaching, 3
Relationship between reading and
    writing, 75
  with composing, 95
  crossover strategies, 76
  promote literacy strategies, 76
  reading like a reader versus like a
    writer, 44
  relationship of helping, 23
  relationship with mechanics, 43
  similar standards, 49
  through stories, 44
  transfer, 97–99
Reluctant or hesitant writers, 3, 35, 41, 66
Repetition, 2

Researching, 45
"Reserved" (Armantrout), 142
Resiliency, 6
Restless desire to arrive at solution, 81
Reverse of the natural storytelling
    process, 61
Revisiting stories, 44
Reyes, María de la Luz, 28, 38, 54, 64,
    83, 95
Rhythm and flow, 116
Richgels, D. J., 18

Samway, Katharine, 29, 38, 54, 64
Say, Allen, 61
Scaffolding, 2, 15, 26, 30, 61
Scaffolding Young Writers (Dorn &
    Soffos), 112. See also Scaffolding
School language, 109
Sea of talk, 16
Second grade, 87
Secondhand content, 80
Secrets of style, 86
Self-expression, 79–80
Self-monitoring and revisiting texts, 87
Sense of ownership, 6, 64, 75
Sense of voice, 6
Sensitive guidance, 53
Sentences, 49, 82, 84
Shaping at the point of utterance,
    17–18, 48, 94
Sight words, 84
Significance of first drafts, 81
Simon, Neil, 5
Six principles of writing and drawing, 22
Small moments, 67, 99
Sociocultural and linguistic roots, 26
Soffos, Carla, 112
Sondheim, Stephen, 8, 43
Sound-symbol correspondence, 5, 18
Spanish, 48, 54, 117, 131
Spelling, 2, 5, 18, 19, 20, 69
Spontaneity in writing, 17, 58
Standards as signposts, 36–37

Story arc, 2
Story mountain, 96, 97, 98, 122
Storybooks, 83
Stratta, Leslie, 69
Strengthening connections on the spot, 69
Stretching out the problem, 98
Stribling, Stacia, 35, 85
Strong leads, 91
Structured lessons, 65
Stubb, Michael, 109
Style, 3, 6, 51
Support for young writers, 2, 38, 54, 64
Symbol users and symbol weavers, 27, 58
Synergy, 30
Syntactical structures, 5, 17, 83

Taking risks, 80
Teachable moments, 26
Teacher supported format, 83
Teachers
    being engaged, 139
    development of career, 41
    editing and revision challenges, 101
    as editor in chief, 112
    expectations, 34
    modeling writing, 66, 112, 141–143
    role of, 2–3, 4, 25, 27, 36, 79
    voice, 12
Teachers College Reading and Writing
    Project, The, 25
Teaching mind, 11, 32, 46, 135,
    138–143
Teberosky, Ana, 21, 40
Telling truths, 79
Text structure, 26
Thinking out loud, 59
Third grade, 43, 75
Thoughts to speech, 15
Time, 4, 7, 20, 44
Toolbox of strategies and knowledge, 80
Tower, Wells, 53
Tse, Florence, 10, 37, 54, 73, 83
Turbill, J., 18

Ugly Vegetables, The (Lin), 104
Units of meaning, 38
Units of study curriculum, 25–26
Unspoken messages, 22

van der Rol, R., 6
Varied texts, 22
Vida, Vendela, 52–53
Visual links of reading and writing, 97
Visualization to integrate content and
    mechanics, 88
Vocabulary words, 69, 83, 89
Vygotsky, Lev, 14, 28, 30, 38, 41,
    48, 57, 58, 59, 80. See also
    Scaffolding; Zone of proximal
    development

"Why Couldn't Snow White Be
    Chinese" (Lin), 148
Withers, Bill, 81
Wolf's Chicken Stew, The (Kasza), 91
Wondrous Words (Ray), 44
Woolf, Virginia, 52
Word bank, 19
Word choice, 39–40, 69
Writer's Diary, A (Woolf), 52
Writer's notebook, 46, 60, 67, 75
Writer's workshops, 44–46, 93
Writing as a craft, 24, 25, 41, 49, 107
    as a dance, 8, 9, 13, 87
Writing conferences, 43
Writing instruction, 32
Writing journey, 20
Writing mind, 8, 9, 48, 52, 134,
    138–139
Writing process approach, 25, 91
Writing rehearsal, 63
Writing setbacks, 6
Writing that makes a difference, 78

Zone of proximal development, 15, 48,
    57, 93–94. See also Vygotsky, Lev;
    Scaffolding

ABOUT THE AUTHOR

Daniel Meier is professor of elementary education at San Francisco State University, and teaches courses on children's first and second language and literacy learning, narrative inquiry and memoir, and teacher research. Professor Meier holds degrees from Wesleyan University, Harvard University, and the University of California at Berkeley. He has worked with preschool and elementary school children on literacy development, and with teachers on inquiry-based projects at the early childhood and elementary school levels. He is the author of numerous books on education published by Teachers College Press, and is also co-editor of *Voices of Practitioners*, an online journal solely devoted to publishing teacher research in early childhood education. He lives in Berkeley, California, with his wife and two children.